BUIL
Be
STUDY SKILLS

BUILDING *Better* STUDY SKILLS

Practical Methods for Succeeding in College

The American College Testing Program
Iowa City, Iowa

ACT Study Skills Coordinating Committee

JoAnn Bowlsbey, DISCOVER Center
Connie Brinton, Educational Services Division
Joan Laing, Research Division, *Coordinator, 1987-88*
Michael McFadden, Publications Department
Terry McNabb, Research Division, *Coordinator, 1988-89*
Cathy Welch, Test Development Division

Consultants

Dr. William F. Brown
Professor of Psychological Services, Department of Educational Administration and Psychological Services, Southwest Texas State University

Dr. Joseph A. Fisher
Professor, Graduate School of Education, Director, Reading and Study Skills Clinic, Drake University

Lea Hinz, M.S.
Coordinator of Reading and Study Skills, Student Counseling Service, Iowa State University

Dr. Thomas Rocklin
Associate Professor, Department of Psychological and Quantitative Foundations, College of Education, University of Iowa

Dr. John N. Schacht
Librarian III, University Libraries, University of Iowa

Dr. James M. Towers
Chair, Division of Education, Saint Mary's College, Winona, Minnesota

Mary E. Wilson, M.A.
Coordinator, Writing Program, Communication Arts Department, Kirkwood Community College, Cedar Rapids, Iowa

Production Team—ACT Publications Department

Jeanette Corpman, *Compositor*
John Laing, *Graphic Artist*
Michael McFadden, *Writer-Editor & Project Manager*
Dean Thomas, *Designer*

Library of Congress Cataloging-in-Publication Data

Building better study skills

Includes index.
1. Study, Method of. 2. Education, Higher.
I. American College Testing Program.
LB2395.B8 1989 378'.1702812 88-33308
ISBN 0-937734-74-8

ACT study skills texts, computer software, and evaluative instruments are based in part on the Effective Study Materials series originated and formerly published by Dr. William F. Brown, who has consulted with ACT on the development of its study skills program.

Contents

Introduction

College isn't just harder than high school. It's fundamentally different. For that reason, college requires students to make major adjustments in their study-related skills, habits, and attitudes. Whether you attend a two-year college or a four-year college or university, whether you're a freshman or an upperclassman, whether you're academically gifted or of average abilities, *Building Better Study Skills* can help you make those adjustments successfully. The same is true whether you're a traditional-age college student or a student beginning or resuming college later in life.

As its subtitle makes clear, this book focuses on *practical methods* for achieving personal and academic success in college. Although some of the study tips presented here are derived from research, the great majority of them are based on the actual study practices of students who have made the grade in college. The suggestions in this book are "real world" solutions that have paid off for other students—and can do so for you.

Building Better Study Skills devotes a separate chapter to each of five skill areas that are vital to success in college.

- Managing Time and Environment
- Reading Textbooks
- Taking Class Notes
- Using Information Resources
- Preparing for and Taking Examinations

Each chapter begins with a Self-Help Checklist that gets you started on analyzing your present strengths and weaknesses in the skill area. A short text then shows you, in step-by-step fashion, *what to do* and *how to do it* in order to build your skills in the area. The text includes just enough information on *why to do it* to satisfy your curiosity about the reasons for, or benefits of, the suggested study methods.

Each chapter features two or more Skill Builder exercises that give you an opportunity to practice some of the study strategies and techniques described here. In all, 12 Skill Builders are included. Extra Skill Builder forms and worksheets are provided in the back of the book.

Building Better Study Skills could be one of the most important books you'll read this year. Whether you're using the book on your own or in a study skills course or workshop, it can help you improve your study skills and habits and your attitudes about college and studying. It can help you enjoy college more, manage your independence better, and get a real education rather than just a degree. If your grades are lower than you'd like, the book can help you gradually raise them.

Of course, as with any other new skill, building better study skills takes time, effort, and practice. If you're willing to work hard at applying them, the suggestions in this book will work for you.

Chapter 1

Managing Time and Environment

Warm-Up

Do your classes and studying leave you too little time for other activities? Have you ever felt that there aren't enough hours in a day to do all the things that ought to be done?

Do you sometimes put off major assignments until the last possible minute—even though you know from experience that you'll regret it?

Does your mind wander when you're trying to write a research paper or review your lecture notes for an exam?

Have you ever looked up from a textbook to realize that you've just "read" a page without having the least idea of what it was about?

If you're like the majority of college students, you could probably answer "Yes" to one or more of those questions. Most students have trouble finding time for all of the things that they need to do and would like to do. Many put off work on papers and other big assignments until just before the due date, even though they keep meaning to get an early start. And some find it hard to study effectively. They just can't settle down and concentrate on a task.

Of course, on every college campus there are also students who have overcome such problems. These students have learned how to turn in their papers and other assignments on time and how to prepare without panic for tests, midterm exams, and finals. These students get the best grades that they're capable of—whether A's, B's, or C's—and generally seem to be making the most of college. They keep up with their assignments and still have time for dating, jobs, campus activities, and day-to-day chores like doing their laundry.

To be sure, some super-efficient students are academically gifted. What characterizes most super-efficient students, though, is a high degree of personal organization. If you've ever wanted to become more organized, this chapter will show you how.

Overview and Benefits

As its title makes clear, this chapter is about managing time and environment. The first section of the chapter offers a three-part look at what college students need to know about time management. The section begins with ten general tips for managing study time. It also features suggestions on planning for the academic term and planning for the academic week. The second section of the chapter examines ways of managing both your physical environment and your "psychological environment." Three Skill Builder exercises are included in the chapter to help you start applying what you learn here.

Managing time and managing environment aren't just study skills. They're valuable *life skills.* When you manage your time and environment effectively, you gain more control over your life. No matter what you do or where you go after college, your chances for success and personal satisfaction will depend in part on your ability to manage your time and environment.

There are probably dozens of ways that improving your skills in managing time and environment can make your life better. Here are just a few of them.

- You'll be more organized and get more done, both as a student and in your other present and future roles.
- You'll learn more from your courses, understand the material in greater depth, and remember and recall it more effectively. You may improve your grades, especially if they don't reflect your true abilities.
- If you're going on to graduate or professional school, you'll have a head start on meeting the increased demands that will be placed on your time.
- You'll develop efficient mental habits that will enhance your performance in future employment. In addition, you'll be better able to handle the conflicts that may sometimes arise if you combine family responsibilities with your career.
- When you finish the things that you *must* do, you'll still have time and energy for the things that you *want* to do.

Checking Your Present Skills

The following Self-Help Checklist will get you started on understanding your present skills, habits, and attitudes related to management of your time and environment. The checklist consists of ten statements.

Read each statement carefully and then mark your answer. Circle the letter "T" if the statement is *true* for you. Circle "F" if the statement is *false* for you. Be honest with yourself. The checklist isn't a test, and there are no "right" or "wrong" answers. Be sure to respond to all ten statements.

Self-Help Checklist:
Managing Time and Environment

---

1. **T F** I often have so many other things going on that it's hard to find time for studying.
2. **T F** I usually study with the TV on.
3. **T F** My usual study area has a work surface big enough for me to spread out my books and papers.
4. **T F** I spend more time studying now than I did in high school.
5. **T F** I often turn in papers or reports late.
6. **T F** I usually study at regular times.
7. **T F** I try to write down course assignments as my instructors announce them.
8. **T F** I have a few specific places where I usually study.
9. **T F** Other people around me often make so much noise that it's hard for me to study.
10. **T F** I usually review for the first time on the night before a test.

- Statements 3, 4, 6, 7, and 8 are almost always *true* for students with good skills and habits in managing time and environment and positive attitudes about the process.
- Statements 1, 2, 5, 9, and 10 are almost always *false* for students with good skills and habits in managing time and environment and positive attitudes about the process.

What Do You Need to Work On?

Each statement in the Self-Help Checklist is based on a specific skill, habit, or attitude with which many college students have trouble. Look back over your answers to see how they compare with the key below the checklist.

As you do so, reread the ten statements. This chapter can help you with all of the matters covered in the checklist—and quite a few more. Ask yourself whether any of your skills, habits, or attitudes related to managing time and environment could stand some strengthening.

Setting Your Goals

By now you may be getting some ideas about what you want to accomplish in this chapter. Use the blanks on this page to write down three goals that you have for the chapter.

The goals that you choose can be related to your academic work or to your personal, social, and recreational activities. Your goals can grow out of your answers to the Self-Help Checklist or out of your thinking about the benefits of improved skills in managing time and environment. Just make sure that the goals you write down are realistic and *personally important* to you.

For example, one of your goals might be "I will make an early start the next time a paper is assigned in class." Another goal could be "I will set aside a few minutes every night, after studying, for personal reading or just plain unwinding."

Where appropriate, word your goals in a way that will allow you to measure your progress. For instance, write down "I will study physics for two more hours during each of the next four weeks" rather than "I will study physics more."

GOAL 1: ______________________________

____

____

GOAL 2: ______________________________

____

____

GOAL 3: ______________________________

____

____

Were you able to think of three goals? Even if you wrote down only one goal, you now have a personal reason for improving your skills in managing time and environment. Keep your reason or reasons in mind as you progress through this chapter. That way, the material will have greater relevance to you, and you'll find it easier to maintain your interest. If you think of more goals later, return to the previous page and add them to your list. Or simply record them wherever you happen to be in the chapter.

Managing Time

Managing time is largely a matter of planning the things that you need to do and setting aside time to do them. If you want to be a more organized person and a better, more efficient student, you have to plan ahead. You have to put yourself on a schedule.

Actually, college students need *two kinds* of schedules. They need a long-range schedule for the academic term and all of the checkpoints along the way, and a short-range schedule for the academic week.

Some students have negative feelings about time management and, in particular, about the idea of scheduling their activities. They think of scheduling as a restrictive process that turns people into robots mechanically "living their lives by the clock." In fact, few misunderstandings could be further from the truth. The purpose of scheduling and other time management techniques is to achieve *freedom*—the kind of freedom that comes only to those who take active control of the ways that they spend their time and effort.

This section will show you how to schedule your studies and other activities both for the academic term and for the academic week. First, though, here are some general tips for effective day-to-day management of your study time.

Ten Tips for Managing Your Study Time

1. Keep a Daily Activity List

To manage your time well, you have to be constantly aware of what needs to be done and in what order. Time management experts suggest writing out a daily list of activities and other responsibilities. Some of the most successful, high-energy leaders in business, government, education, and other fields make it a habit to keep a daily activity list. Keeping such a list can produce results for you, too.

Although it's a matter of personal preference, your daily activity list probably could leave out your regular and scheduled activities such as eating and sleeping, classes, or a job. You aren't likely to forget those activities. The main purposes of a daily activity list are to remind you of all of the other, unscheduled things that need to be done and to help you set some priorities for doing them. When you keep a daily activity list and use it regularly, you'll get more done each day and waste less time. For instance, when you unexpectedly find yourself with 40 minutes of spare time, you'll be less likely to just kill the time. If you check your list, you'll probably find one or more activities that can be easily accomplished during the 40 minutes.

Skill Builder 1 provides a form that makes it simple for you to keep and use a daily activity list. You can also write out a daily activity list on a page in one of your notebooks, on a portable calendar, or on a small slip of paper that you carry in your pocket or purse. At a minimum, your list should include all of your study goals for the day. A more detailed list might also include your personal and extracurricular activities, especially any responsibilities that you might forget or be tempted to put off.

Some students write their most important activities at the top of the list and their less important ones at the bottom. Other students list their activities in random order and then number or letter them from most to least important. List *your* activities in whatever way works best for you. Above all, carry your activity list with you and refer to it often so that you'll always be making the best use of your time and energy.

2. Set Regular Times to Study

Set a few regular times for studying and stick with them. Many college students lose valuable time by studying only in the evening, after dinner. Depending on your living arrangements, course schedule, and nonacademic commitments, there may be several times during the day when you can and should study. For instance, if you have no early morning classes on Tuesday and Thursday, you could sleep a *little* later and still get in an extra hour or two of studying on each of those mornings.

By studying at a few regular times, you'll make studying a productive habit. Just as you become hungry at certain times by force of habit, you can also form strong expectations to study and concentrate at certain times. As you build the habit of studying, you'll notice that you waste less time and mental energy on deciding whether to study, on complaining about studying, and on inventing excuses to avoid studying.

You'll find it easier and perfectly natural to shift into the high-energy frame of mind that studying requires. As a result, you'll concentrate better and learn more. You'll remember the material longer and more clearly and recall it more effectively on exams. Aside from the benefits that you'll enjoy now in college, you'll also be forming good work habits for any advanced education that you undertake and for future employment.

3. Take One Hour at a Time

No matter how much studying you have, you can get it all done by taking it one hour at a time. Think back to an occasion when you got through a difficult task, one that may have looked impossible at first. Remember how you got the job done? Quite likely, it was by starting with a series of small, manageable steps.

The same strategy can help you avoid procrastination when you have an "impossible" amount of studying to do. Don't worry about the fact that there may be three or four hours of work ahead of you. Instead, make a start right away and concentrate on *this* hour's studying. Don't daydream, don't feel sorry for yourself, don't watch the clock, and don't allow any interruptions. Just focus on the work at hand. Remember that your purpose is to study and nothing else. If necessary, give yourself a brief pep talk. Tell yourself that you *can* do it, and that you will.

Before you realize, the hour will be up. If you've been studying effectively, you'll be encouraged to see how much you've accomplished. Treat yourself to a short break. Get up and stretch your legs. Do some exercises. Have a quick snack. Set a definite time limit, though. Five or ten minutes should be about right. Then go back to your desk or carrel and see how much studying is left. If it still seems like a lot, remember to take one hour at a time.

4. Study Each Subject Often

Research has shown that studying a subject for a short time every day (or nearly every day) works much better than studying it for a long time once in a while. This is especially true of courses that are hard to learn. In some ways, learning an academic subject is like learning a new motor skill. If you've ever played a musical instrument or participated in team sports, then you know that frequent practice is the key to becoming skilled. There's really no other way.

Studying involves the same principle. You'll learn a subject better if you study it for one hour four or five times a week than if you study it for four or five hours once a week. The problem with long, infrequent study sessions is that tiredness and boredom eventually set in and reduce your ability to learn the material. So study for each of your courses often, even if some of them meet only once or twice a week. The material will be much easier to understand and remember this way. As a result, you'll probably notice that you're becoming more interested in your courses and developing more positive feelings about them.

5. Keep Pace Every Day

No matter how good your high school education was, or how effective your study practices were, you may be finding that one of your greatest challenges in college is keeping up with the amount of work that your instructors assign. Some of the previous time management tips—like setting regular times to study and studying each subject often—hint at the importance of keeping pace with your studies.

Keeping pace is worth more than a hint, though. If you want to survive and succeed in college, you *must* keep pace with your studies every day. If you don't, you may be unable to understand lectures and class discussions. If you can't follow what's going on in class, you'll soon find yourself in academic difficulty. While college instructors will attempt to help the student who's having trouble keeping up, they are less likely to spoon-feed students than high school teachers are.

In addition, there's the cumulative effect of failing to keep pace with your studies. A week of neglecting your readings, problems, or other assignments can result in a huge amount of material to catch up on. Let things slide for two weeks, and the situation could become overwhelming.

6. Know Your Strengths and Weaknesses

Each student is unique. You differ from your classmates in many ways, including your strengths and weaknesses as a student. Get to know your academic strengths and weaknesses. Adjust your study habits to compensate in the areas where you're not as strong as you'd like to be.

For example, suppose that your math course is very hard for you. One way of dealing with that would be to spend extra time studying for it. Where do you get the extra time? Perhaps from another subject. If your psychology course is fairly easy for you, then you could probably spend less time on that subject and more time on your math, where you need it most. The extra study time will pay off with a better understanding of math and possibly a better grade. Be careful, though. Don't cut back too much on your "good" subject. You want to do better in math *without* slipping in psychology.

7. Don't Forget to Review

Have you ever looked at some class notes three weeks after you took them and realized that the material no longer makes sense? Most likely, the problem was that you didn't *review* the notes earlier.

Reviewing is different from studying material that's new to you. Reviewing is going over material that you've already studied to make sure you've learned it and will be able to recall it when you need to. One of the biggest mistakes that many students make is that they seldom review until just before an exam. This isn't just a poor study habit. It's also a major time management problem. If you don't review until the night before an exam, you'll probably find that there's far too much material to cover in the time left to you. Also, you may discover that you didn't really learn the material very well in the first place.

You can avoid those problems by making review a part of your regular study schedule. Ideally, you should review for each of your courses right after class. If that isn't possible, make it a point to review for each course at least once a week. Go over all of your readings and class notes for the entire week and make sure that you really understand the material.

An even better procedure is to begin each study session by reviewing the previous textbook assignment and class notes for that course. Don't just look back and turn pages, though. Quiz yourself to make sure that you know the material. To be effective, reviewing must be an active, questioning process.

When you review regularly, you'll begin to see how the main ideas connect in each of your courses. Seeing these connections can help you understand and remember the material better. Also, reviewing gives you a chance to spot trouble early. If you find that you don't know some of the material as well as you thought you did, you'll still have time to ask questions in class or see the instructor during office hours before you're tested on the material. You'll also have time to get things cleared up if you notice that the textbook and the instructor don't agree on a major point.

8. Use Your Spare Time for Studying

A college student's day is full of many short intervals of spare time. Because intervals of 15 minutes here or 40 minutes there don't *seem* long enough to do much with, many students waste them. Added up, though, the spare time in a college student's day could total two or three hours or more.

In fact, your spare time isn't "spare" at all. If you want to keep up with your assignments and turn in the best work that you're capable of, you must get into the habit of using those odd moments and hours for studying and review. An hour or two of nightly studying may have been enough in high school, but in college you'll almost certainly have to devote more time to your studies than that.

For example, if you have an hour between morning classes, why not put it to good use instead of walking around or watching TV? With that hour, you could go over your notes from your previous class and get a good start on the assigned reading or other work. As an alternative, you could review for your next class that morning.

If you commute to classes, see if you can get some studying or reviewing done during the drive. Some students use commuting time to listen to tapes of lectures that they recorded earlier. Other good chances to study or review include any time you might spend waiting at a laundromat, riding the campus bus, or standing in lines.

Use the weekends for studying, too. Set aside some time, perhaps on Sunday afternoon or early on Sunday evening, to review the past week's work and get ready for the week ahead. Catch up on any assignments that you've fallen behind on. Weekends are also a good time to work on research papers and other projects that require large blocks of time or use of library reference materials.

9. Keep Your Balance

Although your studies must be your top priority in college, it's important to maintain a comfortable balance between academic work and your other interests. Certainly, you need to allow enough time for classes and studying. If you expect to keep your mind and body healthy, though, you also need time for eating, sleeping, recreation, dating, and all the other things you do that aren't directly related to your studies.

Most colleges offer a wealth of extracurricular activities and resources. Explore what's available on your campus and in the community. Get involved with a *few* carefully selected groups or activities that will complement your academic training and help you to grow as a person.

10. Trade Time When You Need To

When something happens that throws you off your study schedule, like a weekend trip, a visit from an old friend, or a campus event that you can't afford to miss, decide right away how you're going to make up the study time you've lost. Don't just ignore the matter. If you do that, you're letting events control you. The purpose of putting yourself on a schedule is for *you* to control events.

Your best bet is to trade for some study time. In other words, use some of the time you've set aside for recreation or other personal interests to make up the lost study time. Clearly, you won't want to do this too often, because your personal time is very important. When you really need to make up lost study time, though, you should be willing to trade. After all, even if you're employed, studying is your full-time "job" while you're in college.

Summary:
Ten Tips for Managing Your Study Time

1. Keep a daily activity list and use it as a guide for getting the important things done on time.
2. Develop a highly productive study habit by setting regular times to study and sticking to them.
3. Study in blocks of an hour or so at a time, each followed by a short break.
4. Study for each course several times a week.
5. Keep pace with your assignments.
6. Know your strengths and weaknesses as a student and put extra time and effort on the courses you find hardest.
7. Review for each of your courses *at least* once a week.
8. Use your spare time—especially time between classes—and weekends for studying and review.
9. Maintain a healthy balance between your studies and your other activities and interests.
10. Trade off some of your recreation time when you need to make up study time that you've lost.

Skill Builder 1:
Making a Daily Activity List

This Skill Builder will show you how to organize your daily activities by listing them and assigning priorities to them.

INSTRUCTIONS

- Look at the filled-in Daily Activity List on the next page. Notice the kinds of activities that are listed under each of the three headings.
- Think of all the activities that you need to do and want to do tomorrow.
- Write your activities for tomorrow on the blank Daily Activity List on page 24. Put each activity under one of the three headings on the list according to the importance of the activity.
  - "Must Do!"—Activities that you *are required* to do or *need* to do.
  - "Should Do"—Activities that you *ought* to do but can delay for a while.
  - "Could Do"—Activities that you *might like* to do if you have time.

  In deciding which of your activities to list, you may find it helpful to review the section on "Keep a Daily Activity List" (pages 13-14).
- Tomorrow, use your activity list as a guide for getting the most important things done on time. Check off each activity as you do it. Try to check off all of the "Must Do!" activities and a good mix of the "Should Do" and "Could Do" activities.
- Using the extra blank activity lists in Appendix A of this book, continue filling out and following a list every day. (Leave one activity list blank for making photocopies.) Try for steady, gradual improvement. Don't be discouraged if some activities remain undone at the end of a day. Remember, though, to get your "Must Do!" activities done each day even if that means delaying some of your less important activities.

Daily Activity List for Tuesday 27th
day

MUST DO!

1. See Ms. Trice re. Math probs. for Fri.
2. Catch up on History reading
3. Birthday card to Mom (call over weekend)
4. Get Spanish-English dictionary
5. ▶ milk, cereal, apples, felt-tip marker (blue)
6.
7.
8.

SHOULD DO

1. Library: Start research for English paper
2. Laundry
3. Lend Chem. lab notes to Pat
4. Pick up concert tickets
5.
6.
7.
8.

COULD DO

1. Call Chris re. homecoming game and dance
2. Get 360K diskettes
3. Sign up for intramurals
4.
5.
6.
7.
8.

Daily Activity List for ______________________
day

MUST DO!

1. ______________________
2. ______________________
3. ______________________
4. ______________________
5. ______________________
6. ______________________
7. ______________________
8. ______________________

SHOULD DO

1. ______________________
2. ______________________
3. ______________________
4. ______________________
5. ______________________
6. ______________________
7. ______________________
8. ______________________

COULD DO

1. ______________________
2. ______________________
3. ______________________
4. ______________________
5. ______________________
6. ______________________
7. ______________________
8. ______________________

Planning for the Academic Term

Another important time management skill is making long-range plans. Unfortunately, it's a skill that many new college students haven't fully developed, perhaps because they didn't need to in high school. Among the ways in which college differs most from high school—along with the increased volume and complexity of the academic work—is that college courses typically require fewer but bigger "products" (exams, papers, etc.).

When you were in high school, your grade in a subject may have been based on 12 to 15 weekly quizzes and several short papers or reports. In a college course, the required products usually will be spaced further apart than in high school, and each will represent a larger proportion of your grade. In many college courses, grades are based solely on a midterm exam, a final exam, and perhaps a major term paper or research report.

College also differs from high school in the amount of freedom that students are allowed—personal freedom, intellectual freedom, freedom to succeed or fail as they choose. If you tend to put off work on tasks with distant completion dates, you're likely to experience a shock in college. If you procrastinate, if you can't seem to find the starting point on major projects until just before they're due, you may find it surprisingly easy to slide into difficulty.

This section can help you make the adjustments necessary to overcome any unproductive time management habits you may have acquired in high school. You'll learn how to plan for an entire academic term, so you can keep track of major assignments like midterms, finals, and research papers—and make steady progress toward turning in your best work when those distant due dates come around.

The key to planning for the academic term is to draw up a long-range schedule. The schedule should show, for each of your major assignments, both the due date set by your instructor and the intermediate goals that you'll need to reach along the way. Keeping a long-range schedule for the academic term helps you divide big assignments like research papers into small, manageable tasks (your intermediate goals) such as picking a topic, going to the library, and starting to locate sources of information. There are six steps in planning for the academic term.

1. Learn the Academic Policies and Deadlines

All colleges have policies governing students' course loads, majors, academic standing, and so forth. The policies usually are described in the college catalog, freshman/transfer handbook, or orientation guide. Make sure that you know about all of the academic policies that can affect you.

For instance, whether or not you've picked your major, you should have a good idea of the number of credit hours typically required for the degree you're seeking. You should also know the grade point average and number of credits required to remain in good standing and advance from one academic term to the next. Finally, you should know the core courses that you'll be required to take, and the maximum and minimum course loads.

Don't feel that you have to take the maximum course load. The freshman year of college can be a challenge, even for very able students. Often, students who breezed through high school with little difficulty overextend themselves as college freshmen by taking an extra course. For the great majority of freshmen enrolled in full-time studies, it makes good sense to take the "typical" or standard course load. In this way, you'll have a better chance of successfully making the needed adjustments in your study habits and surviving your freshman year.

You should also know your school's academic deadlines. Almost all colleges have deadlines for students to drop or add courses, switch course sections, and make similar changes. At most schools, students can't add a course after the first two or three weeks of a term. It would be too difficult for a new student to catch up with the other students in the course. Schools often have *two* deadlines for dropping courses. If you miss the first deadline, you may forfeit a partial refund of your tuition for the course. Miss the second deadline, and you may have to take a failing grade in the course.

While every student should be aware of such academic deadlines, they're crucial for freshmen and transfer students, who may need to make emergency changes if they find that they've registered for the wrong course—or too many courses. The important academic deadlines at your college probably are listed in the same publications that describe the school's general academic policies. Make sure that you know and understand the policies and deadlines that apply to you. If you're uncertain, check with a reliable source, such as the campus advising center or the registrar's office.

2. Set Your Academic Goals

Another important step in planning for the academic term is to think about what you want to accomplish during the term—what you want to learn, what grades you want to achieve. Write down the names and numbers of your courses and the grade that you want to earn in each of them. Give some thought to the grades you want before you write them down. Ask yourself what grades you'll *need* in order to keep your educational options open.

For instance, if you're considering graduate or professional school, or if you want to qualify for an honors program or a competitive major, then grades will be very important in establishing your eligibility. Grades are also important to get and keep financial aid of almost any kind. Whatever your situation, think realistically about your strengths and weaknesses as a student. Then challenge yourself by setting your academic goals just a little higher than what you think would be easy to reach.

3. Find Some Study Partners

To succeed in college, you'll probably need to devote more time to studying than to any other activity, with the possible exception of sleeping. Much of your studying can be done only when you're alone. At times, though, you may find it helpful to study with a partner. *Cooperative studying,* as this is called, might not work very well for you with your best friend or the person you're dating. It would be too easy to forget that you're supposed to be studying.

A better idea would be to ask a person in one (or more) of your courses whether he or she would like to give cooperative studying a try. If you do try it, some ground rules will be in order. Most obviously, you'll both need to agree that studying is your first and only priority. In addition, you'll need to agree on a procedure. Here's a strategy that can work well for study partners who want to prepare for an examination together.

1. Both students silently review the material to be covered and identify likely exam questions.
2. One student asks a question of the other.
3. Without looking at notes or textbook, the second student responds aloud to the question.
4. The questioner—referring to notes or textbook as needed—points out errors or omissions and adds thoughts of his or her own.
5. After any discussion necessary to decide on the best response to the question, both students add supplemental information to their notes, if desired.
6. The students then reverse roles, with the second student asking a question of the first.

If you think that cooperative study sessions might help you, try to find a partner who is just as serious as you are about learning the subject matter and who shares your interest in experimenting with cooperative studying.

Your study partner probably doesn't have to be at your exact level in terms of grades or ability. Cooperative study can benefit both partners even when they have different ability levels. The less able student can benefit from the explanations and insights of the more able student. The more able student can benefit from the act of thinking out and explaining the material.

There's another plus in having a study partner. If you need to miss a class, you can copy notes from your partner and find out what reading or other work was assigned.

4. Record All Exams

As your instructors announce them, write down the dates, topics, and page assignments for all tests and examinations. Later, when you get back to your room or apartment, transfer the information from your class notes to a wall calendar or desk calendar. Use a calendar that has large boxes for the days of the month and refer to it often so you'll see important exam dates well in advance. This will help you to get an early start on exam preparation.

Also write down on your calendar the *type* of examination your instructor announces—essay, objective, problem-solving, or other. (As you'll learn in Chapter 5, Preparing for and Taking Examinations, the type of exam will have an effect on what and how you study.) Then write down the score or letter grade that you want to achieve on each exam.

Finally, back up from each exam date and schedule the date by which you'll need to finish your readings and other assignments and begin your intensive review. Allow yourself plenty of time. Don't make the mistake of thinking that the last-minute cram sessions that work for many students in high school will do the job in college. Chances are, they won't. For a small test or a lab quiz, you may find that you need to start your review two or three days in advance. For midterms and final exams, two or three *weeks* in advance isn't too early to start reviewing.

5. Record Other Assignments

As your instructors announce them, write down the topics and due dates for all other major assignments, such as compositions and research papers. Write down any rules or suggestions that your instructors make. For instance, if an instructor says that your paper should be 3,000 words long or should draw on scholarly journal articles, write it down so you'll remember. Also write down any guidelines the instructor provides about the style that you should follow in typing a paper for his or her course.

Then transfer the key details to your calendar. You'll have room for the information if your calendar has a large box for each day. Also, record the score or the letter grade that you want to earn on each assignment. Last, estimate the amount of preparation time you'll need and schedule a realistic date by which to start work on the assignment.

6. Monitor Your Calendar—and Your Performance

Check your deadlines and due dates every day. This will help you to get an early start on the major efforts required for exams, papers, and other big assignments. It will also help you to keep pace with your day-to-day studying. If you set aside a catch-up study period on the weekend, that's an excellent time to check on important dates. When you get into the habit of keeping and monitoring an assignments calendar, you'll always know what major projects are coming due or should be started on during the weeks ahead. Then, as you plan for the next week, you can build in the extra time you'll need for those projects.

When your instructors return your completed exams and other assignments, look them over carefully and note the grades that you received. Comparing your actual grades to the goals you set for each course will show you where you're putting in enough time and effort—and where you need to work harder. You might find that, for especially difficult courses, you need to schedule your preparation for exams and other assignments even further in advance.

When you miss questions on an exam or lose points on a paper, be sure you understand the reason so you can learn from experience. Pay particular attention to any comments that an instructor writes on your work. If you don't know *why* you've received a lower grade than you expected, or if you feel that you need help with the subject matter of a course, see your instructor during office hours as soon as possible.

Summary:
Planning for the Academic Term

1. Learn all you can about the academic policies and deadlines that might affect your chances for success in college.
2. Set specific goals for the grades you want and *need* in each of your courses to keep your educational options open.
3. Find a study partner in one or more of your courses and give cooperative studying a try.
4. Write down all tests and exams as they're announced—including exam date, topics, page assignments, and type of exam. For each exam, determine the grade you want and schedule adequate time for reviewing.
5. Write down all papers and other major assignments as they're announced—including due date, topics, and special rules or suggestions. Determine the grades you want and schedule plenty of preparation time.
6. Check your deadlines and due dates every day and get an early start on big assignments. Compare the grades you receive with the goals you've set and adjust your preparation time, or get academic help, as needed.

Planning for the Academic Week

In addition to making long-range plans for the entire academic term, the ability to make short-range plans for the academic week is another important time management skill for college students. Most students find that keeping pace with their assignments in college requires at least four times as much preparation as in high school. High school students often can get by with a half-hour or less of homework for each hour that they spend in class. In college, a standard rule of thumb is to count on spending two hours or more studying for each hour spent in class.

With that kind of work load, it shouldn't be hard to see that good skills in managing study time—and study effort—are essential for college students. If you want to get better at managing your study time and effort, making a schedule for your typical week can be an excellent way of doing so.

To be effective, a weekly schedule should:

- Cover all recurring, major demands on your time, both academic and personal.
- Account for every day of the week, including Saturday and Sunday, and every hour of each day.
- Be flexible enough for you to deal with unexpected changes.
- Allow you a sensible balance of studying and personal activities.

In Skill Builder 2, you'll get some practice in setting up a weekly schedule of your own.

The weekly activity schedule for one college student is shown in Figure 1.1 on the next page. Take a minute now to look it over. How are your courses and other activities like those of this student? How are yours different? Would the amount of study time scheduled by this student be enough for you?

Weekly Activity Schedule

Name Terry Gibson Date Sept. 8

Time	Monday	Tuesday	Wednesday	Thursday	Friday	Saturday	Sunday	Time
6:00 6:30								6:00 6:30
7:00 7:30	Breakfast	Breakfast	Breakfast	Breakfast	Breakfast	Breakfast		7:00 7:30
8:00 8:30	History	study English	History	Study English	History	Work	Breakfast	8:00 8:30
9:00 9:30	review Hist. / review Math		review Hist. / review Math		review Hist. / review Math		Recreation	9:00 9:30
10:00 10:30	Math	English	Math	English	Math		Church	10:00 10:30
11:00 11:30	Study Math	Lunch	Study Math	Lunch	Study Math	Library Reading		11:00 11:30
12:00 12:30	Lunch	review Spanish	Lunch	review Spanish	Lunch	Lunch	Lunch	12:00 12:30
1:00 1:30	Chemistry	Spanish	Chemistry	Spanish	Chemistry			1:00 1:30
2:00 2:30	P.E.	Chem. Lab	P.E.	Chem. Lab.	P.E.			2:00 2:30
3:00 3:30	Recreation		Recreation		Recreation	Recreation	Recreation	3:00 3:30
4:00 4:30	Work	Work	Work	Work	Work			4:00 4:30
5:00 5:30								5:00 5:30
6:00 6:30	Dinner	Dinner	Dinner	Dinner	Dinner	Dinner	Dinner	6:00 6:30
7:00 7:30	Recreation	Recreation	Recreation	Recreation	Recreation			7:00 7:30
8:00 8:30	Study Chem.	Study English	Study Chem.	Study English	Study Chem.	Date	catch-up studying	8:00 8:30
9:00 9:30	Study History	Study Spanish	Study History	Study Spanish	Study History			9:00 9:30
10:00 10:30								10:00 10:30

Figure 1.1. Weekly Activity Schedule

Before you make your own weekly schedule, you might want to look back at the "Ten Tips for Managing Your Study Time" (pages 13-21). Many of the tips can be helpful in scheduling. You'll also need a quick overview of what's involved in setting up a good, workable weekly schedule. There are seven steps in the process.

1. Record Fixed Activities

First, write down all of the activities that you do more or less "automatically" at fixed times. These include classes, out-of-class activities (like club meetings, sports practice, or music rehearsals), religious services, and so forth. Also include any work-study or other part-time or full-time job that you have.

If you commute to classes from a distance, be sure to schedule that time, too. Although commuting may not seem like a major use of your time, it could add up to several hours a week.

2. Schedule Time for Daily Living Activities

Set aside time for eating, sleeping, bathing, and dressing. Don't underestimate. Together, these activities can take one-third or more of each 24-hour day and, for some students, closer to one-half.

It's especially important to schedule time for sleeping. If you don't, then sleep may become one of your lowest priorities—something that you attend to only when there's nothing more "urgent" to do. Be realistic and schedule your sleep, just as you would any other activity. And don't limit yourself to five or six hours of sleep if you need seven or eight to be at your best.

3. Schedule Recreation Time

Set aside time for dating, sports, personal reading, watching television, and other forms of recreation and relaxation. Read the campus newspaper and keep an eye on bulletin boards so you'll know about concerts, films, athletic events, political rallies, and other extracurricular activities. Remember, though, not to overcommit yourself to these attractions. While you need a healthy balance between studies and recreation, your studies *must* be your highest priority.

4. Schedule Study Time

For each course that you have, schedule time for your studying and other assignments. You may be surprised to see how much time you have left for studying after you've set aside time for your fixed activities, daily living activities, and recreation. Although college students sometimes complain that there isn't enough time to do all of their studying, most students have more than enough time. Their real problem is that they don't use their time effectively.

The amount of time you need to study probably will vary from one course to another. In estimating study time for a particular course, consider the difficulty of the material, your academic background and ability in the subject area, the grade that you want to earn, and how well you study. (As mentioned earlier, you should probably count on two hours or more of studying for each hour that you spend in class.) Do this for each of your courses and mark off the necessary time on your schedule. Don't just write down "STUDY." Write down the name of each course at the times when you plan to study it. Later, this will keep you from wasting valuable study time on deciding what to study.

5. Schedule Review Time

Don't forget to schedule time for regularly reviewing the material that you've studied. On any given day, you're likely to have several hours of spare time—between classes, between your last morning class and lunch, and so forth. Use as much of this time as you can for reviewing the material that's just been covered in class. Set aside some time on weekends for reviewing, for catching up, and for any special projects that you're working on.

6. Build in Time Off

As you schedule your activities for the week, try to build in a little time here and there to reward yourself for a job well done. There's nothing wrong with taking some time off during the week *if* you've been devoting enough time and effort to your studies.

For instance, if there are one or two weeknight television shows that you enjoy, tentatively schedule time to watch them. But make a rule that you will watch your shows only if you can afford the time. Using these conditional rewards as goals, you should find it easier to get motivated and make the most of your study time during the week.

7. Check Your Progress and Adjust Your Schedule

When you've made your weekly schedule and begun to use it, check up on yourself now and then to see how you're doing. Your weekend review session is a good time for that. After you've reviewed for all of your courses and done any catching up that you need, take a few minutes to look back over the week and see how closely you've followed your schedule.

The goal is to have a standard schedule that you can use throughout the academic term. Your schedule should be flexible enough, however, to allow for changes in priorities from one week to the next.

If your schedule doesn't quite work, adjust it to fit your usual weekly requirements. If you still aren't able to follow your schedule, then either it's too demanding, or you need to try harder to stick to it. By looking back over each week, you'll learn from experience and be able to adjust your schedule and your effort if you need to.

Summary:
Planning for the Academic Week

1. Record all of your fixed activities like classes, meetings, religious services, and employment.
2. Set aside enough time for eating, sleeping, bathing, and dressing.
3. Set aside time for dating, sports, campus events, and other forms of recreation.
4. Schedule time to do your studying and other assignments in each of your courses.
5. Schedule time for regularly reviewing the material you've studied.
6. Build in some conditional time off to motivate yourself and to reward yourself for using your study time effectively.
7. Check your progress and adjust your schedule as needed.

Skill Builder 2:
Making a Weekly Activity Schedule

In this Skill Builder, you'll get some firsthand experience in planning and scheduling your academic and other activities for an entire week.

INSTRUCTIONS

- Using the blank Weekly Activity Schedule on the next two pages, write in your activities as described in the text on "Planning for the Academic Week" (pages 32-38).
  1. Record fixed activities.
  2. Schedule time for daily living activities.
  3. Schedule recreation time.
- Now add up all of the time periods that are still empty. The total is the amount of time that you have each week for your studying and reviewing. Write in those activities as described in the text. Remember to plan some conditional time off as a reward.
  4. Schedule study time.
  5. Schedule review time.
  6. Build in time off.
- Follow your schedule for at least a week. Then check your progress and, if necessary, adjust the schedule. Use the extra blank schedule forms in Appendix A. (Save one blank schedule for making photocopies.) You may need to try two or three different versions of your schedule before it's realistic and workable. The goal is to have a schedule that reserves enough time for all of your regular activities but is still flexible enough to let you find time for unexpected events.

Weekly Activity Schedule

Name ______________________________

Time	Monday	Tuesday	Wednesday	Thurs
6:00 6:30				
7:00 7:30				
8:00 8:30				
9:00 9:30				
10:00 10:30				
11:00 11:30				
12:00 12:30				
1:00 1:30				
2:00 2:30				
3:00 3:30				
4:00 4:30				
5:00 5:30				
6:00 6:30				
7:00 7:30				
8:00 8:30				
9:00 9:30				
10:00 10:30				

Date ____________________

...day	Friday	Saturday	Sunday	Time
				6:00 6:30
				7:00 7:30
				8:00 8:30
				9:00 9:30
				10:00 10:30
				11:00 11:30
				12:00 12:30
				1:00 1:30
				2:00 2:30
				3:00 3:30
				4:00 4:30
				5:00 5:30
				6:00 6:30
				7:00 7:30
				8:00 8:30
				9:00 9:30
				10:00 10:30

Managing Environment

Up to this point, you've been exploring ways to get better at managing your study time. The rest of this chapter is about managing your study environment—both your physical environment and your "psychological environment."

Managing Your Physical Environment

Physical environment means your surroundings, the actual places in which you study. When you were in high school, you probably didn't have much choice about where to study. Chances are, you lived with your family and studied at home. In college, though, living arrangements vary greatly—and so do the choices of where to study.

Many college students, especially freshmen and sophomores, live in dormitories on campus. Other students, especially upperclassmen, live in fraternity or sorority houses, student apartment buildings, or rooming houses close to the campus. And some students, especially at two-year colleges, commute from outlying apartments or houses where they live with their friends or families.

Because there's such a variety of living arrangements among college students, no single place for studying can be regarded as best for everyone. There are some generally recognized features, though, of environments that are good for effective studying. The ideal study environment is one that's quiet and private. It has good lighting and ventilation and is neither too hot nor too cool. It has a desk or table that's big enough to let you spread out your study materials. It has a chair and all of the books, supplies, and other materials that you need for studying.

Are the places where you study like that? If not, here are four steps that can help you improve your physical environment for more effective studying.

1. Find Some Regular Places to Study

In the first part of this chapter, you learned how important it is to set aside regular times to study. It's equally important to have one or more regular *places* to study during those times. When you study at regular times and in a few regular places, you're building a productive habit. As a result, studying will become easier for you, and you'll make far better use of your study time and energy.

Many students find that the college library is the best place for studying. That makes a lot of sense. Libraries, after all, are designed and built for scholarly reading, thinking, and writing. They're quiet. They have carrels and large tables. They offer the books and related information resources that college students need for their term papers and other research assignments.

For any given student, though, the suitability of a study location may depend on a number of factors. These factors include the time of day, the point in the academic term, the student's ability to shut out distractions, and the nature of the material being studied. College dormitories, for instance, sometimes are quiet enough for studying in the early morning but are almost always too noisy in the evening and on weekends. The library may be uncrowded most of the time but fill up near midterms and finals.

The point is for you to carefully select a few places where *you* can study effectively. For starters, try the college library. Day in and day out, the library probably will be one of the best places for you to study. The dorm probably will be one of the poorest places to study. If academic buildings are open during the evening on your campus, see whether you can use one of the lecture halls or classrooms for studying. If you're eligible to use a departmental library or reading room, try studying there once in a while—especially when you need access to books or journals specific to that subject area.

For students who live off campus, the choice of study locations is affected by distance. If you live only a short walk or drive from the campus, make a point of doing most of your studying on campus. The facilities there are likely to be far better for studying than those where you live. In addition, by studying on campus you'll stay tuned in to college life and events. This can help you avoid the feelings of alienation that "day students" sometimes have. Skill Builder 3 will show you how to evaluate and compare your study locations.

2. Eliminate Distractions

No matter where you live or study, there are three kinds of distractions that can sidetrack your studying if you let them—sounds, sights, and interruptions. To be at your best when you study, you'll need to identify and eliminate any of the three that are present in your study areas.

- *Sounds*. One of the main benefits of studying in the college library is that the library offers an environment fairly free of distracting sounds. If you try to study where you live, you'll almost certainly have trouble with distracting sounds. The greatest of these distractions are likely to be the radio, the stereo, and the television. The voices and movements of other people also can distract you.

  To reduce distracting sounds when you must study in your living quarters, you might want to suggest "quiet hours" to your roommate(s) or family members. During quiet hours, the students in the group study. Any other people present go about their normal activities but more quietly than usual. Some students find it helpful not to make or receive telephone calls during quiet hours.

Many students feel that music serves as a useful background sound to filter out more distracting noises when they study. In some cases, music really may help. Often, though, students who think that they're studying while there's music playing are just fooling themselves. If you feel that you need music to mask other sounds when you study, by all means give it a try. You'll probably get better results with instrumental music than with vocal music. Song lyrics have a way of capturing your attention without your realizing it. Try some classical music or light jazz, and keep the volume low. If you're consciously aware of the music, you can't be concentrating fully on your studies.

- *Sights.* One of the distractions likely to be found wherever college students live has already been mentioned—the television. Television is both a sound distraction and a sight distraction. Because it appeals to your ears *and* to your eyes, television is one of the most powerful distractions. There's a very simple rule about watching television while you're studying: Don't.

  Try not to face a window or open doorway when you study. If you do, then sooner or later you'll be distracted by things going on outside the window or beyond the doorway. The best way to avoid this is to face a wall when you're studying. Make sure there's nothing on the wall or on your table or desk that could make your mind wander. Ideally, there should be nothing in front of you that's unrelated to studying.

- *Interruptions.* College students often mix studying and socializing. The two activities are incompatible, and, when you mix them, neither works out very well. Learn to draw a clear distinction between studying and socializing. Give your full attention and energy to whichever you are engaged in. For instance, do you sometimes find yourself asking friends, "Are you going to the library tonight? Which floor will you be on?" If so, you're probably mixing studying and socializing. Likewise, if you often look around the library to see who's there, you're not really studying. You're just inviting interruptions.

No matter where you study, the best way to avoid interruptions is to discourage them in advance. You can do this by making it clear through your manner that, during your scheduled study time, you are interested in studying and nothing else. There's no need to be aloof or unpleasant to others. Being *task-oriented* will send the message clearly enough.

If you're studying in a dorm room or in your own bedroom in an apartment or house, close the door and let people know that this signal means you don't want to be disturbed. Even then, you'll probably have to negotiate for good study conditions once in a while. This is most likely to be the case if you share a dorm room or apartment with one or more roommates. Try to work out an arrangement that everyone involved can live with. Quiet hours, mentioned earlier, is one possibility. If you can't work things out, then you're studying in the wrong place. Get to the library and make yourself a regular there.

3. Arrange Your Study Area

You've already seen that each of your usual study places should have a desk or table and a chair. Many college students find that a straight-backed chair is best for studying because it helps them to keep alert and to concentrate fully on their work. Don't try to study in bed or in a soft armchair. You're likely to get too relaxed, and, before long, you may start getting sleepy.

You can use almost any desk or table with a flat, smooth work surface big enough to let you spread out your books and other study materials. Whatever the size of your work surface, don't let it get cluttered. When you sit down to study, clear it of everything that you don't need for the assignment you're working on.

You should have good, even lighting across your work surface. Soft, indirect lighting is better for your eyes than is direct lighting. The temperature and ventilation in your study area are also important. What's best, however, is largely a matter of personal preference. If it's possible for you to control the temperature and ventilation in your study area, adjust them so that you're comfortable and alert.

4. Organize Your Study Materials

The final step in managing your physical environment is to organize your study materials. This step begins during the day in your classes. As you take notes in class, write down your assignments and any other announcements that your instructors make. Doing so will get you *mentally* organized and make it unlikely that you'll forget a key assignment. Also, if an assignment requires special supplies or materials—diskettes, pastels, a style guide for your paper in psychology—you'll have a record of exactly what you need.

When you get back to your dorm room or other living quarters, don't just dump your books on the floor. Stack them neatly on your study surface or close at hand. Put your first assignment on top of the stack. Later, when you begin to study, you won't waste any time figuring out what your priorities should be.

Make sure that your study supplies are well stocked and kept organized. You should have everything that you're likely to need, and all of it should be easy to find. Things that you use often, like a dictionary and pencils, could be on your study desk or table. Things that you use less often, like a stapler and a ruler, should be out of your way but nearby. If you have a desk with drawers, the drawers will come in handy for keeping your supplies organized. Shelves or a small bookcase near your study surface can be helpful, too. At the end of each study session, put everything back where it belongs.

Summary:
Managing Your Physical Environment

1. Develop the study habit by studying in a few regular places.
2. Eliminate the distracting sights, sounds, and interruptions that can interfere with your study concentration.
3. Make sure that your study desk or table, your lighting, your chair, and the temperature and ventilation are suitable for effective studying.
4. Keep your study materials and supplies organized and close at hand.

Skill Builder 3:
Finding Your Best Place to Study

This Skill Builder will help you to compare the places where you study and decide which of them is likely to be your best *place for studying.*

INSTRUCTIONS

- Look at the Study Locations Worksheet on the next two pages. In the boxes labeled "Location A," "Location B," and "Location C," list up to three places where you study.
- As you read each of the 15 numbered statements on the worksheet, make a check mark (✓) under every study location for which the statement is generally true.
- When you've responded to all 15 statements, add up the total number of check marks for each study location. Write your totals at the bottom of the worksheet. The location with the fewest check marks is probably the best place for you to study. The location with the most check marks is probably the most difficult place to study.

From now on, try to do your studying in the place that received the fewest check marks. See whether you notice any improvements in the effectiveness of your studying or in your attitudes toward studying.

If you want to, you may be able to make your best study place even better. To do this, first review any statements that you checked for your best study place. Each statement checked suggests a possible problem in that place. Look back at the section on "Managing Your Physical Environment" (pages 42-48) for ideas about how to reduce or eliminate those problems.

Study Locations Worksheet

When I study here:
1. I am often interrupted or disturbed by other people.
2. I am often reminded of things that have little to do with studying.
3. I can often hear the stereo, radio, or television.
4. I can often hear the telephone ringing.
5. I can often hear other people talking.
6. I tend to take too many breaks from my studying.
7. I tend to spend time talking to others instead of studying.
8. I tend to daydream about things that have little to do with studying.
9. I tend to spend time on the telephone instead of studying.
10. I tend to spend time looking out a window or door instead of studying.
11. I tend to be distracted by people-watching instead of studying.
12. I tend to get involved in things that have little to do with studying.
13. I often find that the temperature and ventilation are not very good for studying.
14. I often find that the furniture and lighting are not very helpful for studying.
15. I often find that needed study materials are elsewhere.

Number of Statements

	Location A Bedroom on Bed	Location B Bedroom on desk	Location C
	✓	✓	
	✓	✓	
	✓	✓	
	✓	✓	
	✓	✓	
	✓	✓	
	✓		
Checked	7	6	

Managing Your "Psychological Environment"

Your psychological environment is made up of the inner conditions that can affect your studying. These conditions include your habits, your attitudes, your ability to concentrate, your self-image, your feelings about your relationships with others, and your reasons for going to college. Managing your psychological environment is probably at least as important as managing your physical environment. After all, if your frame of mind were good enough, you could study almost anywhere.

Unfortunately, one of the most common problems among college freshmen is inability to manage their psychological environment. Difficulty of this kind shows itself in various ways from one freshman to the next. Most new college students experience exhilaration—and with it, perhaps, some anxiety—over the independence that college allows them. That's quite natural.

Some freshmen, though, cannot or will not develop the sense of personal responsibility necessary to manage their new independence. Without the support and gentle chiding of their parents and their high school teachers, they find themselves unable to subordinate their social activities to their studies as college students must. On their own for the first time in life, they prove incapable of keeping up with their studies *and* assuming responsibility for their own budgeting, housekeeping, laundry, meals, and so forth.

Having one or more roommates and learning the process of compromise also can be a big psychological adjustment for many freshmen. Yet another common challenge is the need to develop—or improve on—such personal qualities as self-discipline, concentration, and the ability to stick to a long and complex task. In addition, many freshmen experience homesickness.

It should be no surprise, then, that learning to manage your psychological environment may be harder than learning to manage your physical environment. That's because rearranging your ways of thinking and feeling is a bit more complex than rearranging your desk, chair, lamp, and books. It can be done, though. Four steps are involved.

1. Develop a Positive Attitude

Successful college students accept the fact that, for several years of their lives, studying will be their full-time job. Consequently, they study as much as they need to, whether or not they especially "want to" or "feel like it." That's a sensible, positive attitude to have.

But how do you develop a positive attitude if you don't have one to start with? One way is to set goals for yourself. Form some ideas about what you want to do with your life, what you want to become, and what you need to achieve in college in order to prepare yourself for success. When you have goals of this sort, you'll begin to see the link between the present and the future. You'll see the long-range purpose of what you're doing here and now. When you know the purpose of what you're doing, you're much more likely to enjoy your work and do a good job of it. If the process of establishing plans and goals for the future seems abstract at this point in your life, you might want to visit your school's counseling office or career center. The people there can help you start getting a fix on your future.

There are other good ways to develop a positive attitude. One is to use a strategy called *positive self-talk*. Most people address themselves from time to time—if not aloud, then silently in their conscious thoughts. How do you address yourself? If you tend to address yourself with overly harsh criticism ("Screwed up again, didn't you?") or pessimism ("I'll never get all of this done."), you are not developing a very positive attitude. In fact, you probably have a negative outlook on the world and an unfairly low opinion of yourself. You can start putting all of that behind you by being more positive in your self-talk. Instead of criticizing yourself for occasional small failures or oversights, how about commending yourself for all of the things that you do right? Instead of expecting the worst possible outcome for new challenges and other situations, how about trying some optimism?

Another way to develop a positive attitude is to get more interested in your studies. Try to find something worthwhile and useful in each of your courses, even if it's just a single book, principle, idea, or skill that has personal meaning for you. Notice other students who seem to be genuinely excited about their courses. Talk with them about how they got interested. Also, you might ask some of your instructors what led them into their academic fields.

2. Get Down to Business

Having regular study times and study places can make it a lot easier to start each day's assignments in an efficient manner. So can the habit of writing down your assignments and keeping your study materials organized. However, the real key to getting down to the business of studying is in your mind. When it's time to study, you have to shift into a task-oriented frame of mind and put all other activities and interests temporarily on hold.

It will help if you set learning goals and estimated time requirements for your study sessions. For each of your assignments, decide on the level of mastery you want and the amount of time you should need. Be as specific as you can. "Study three hours" and "read economics until 10:00" aren't ideal goals because they can lull you into thinking that effective studying involves little more than simply putting in your time on the books. A better and more motivating goal would focus closely on the specific outcome that you desire: "Read and understand chapter 3, economics, by 10:00."

When you've set some outcome-oriented goals of this sort, get started without delay and study at an efficient pace. Of course, you don't want to work too fast to really learn the material. Pick up the pace just enough to keep yourself mentally sharp and make every minute count.

Don't wear yourself out by worrying or complaining about the amount of studying ahead of you. Just do it. Each time that you sit down and really study in one of your chosen study spots, you are strengthening a positive mental habit for studying. As a result, you'll find it easier to get into that frame of mind the next time.

3. Train Yourself to Concentrate

There are many reasons that college students—and freshmen, in particular—have trouble concentrating on their studies. Some of the study tips mentioned earlier can help you improve your powers of concentration. Remember to try getting interested in your courses, seeing the purpose and the goal of your education, establishing regular times and places for study, and studying in a task-oriented frame of mind. You'll be much less likely to daydream, for example, if you're *interested* in what you're studying. Getting rid of distractions in your study area will also help you to concentrate better.

Sometimes people have internal distractions. For instance, as noted previously, it's quite normal for college freshmen to suffer from homesickness, especially during the first academic term on campus. Social pressures and roommate problems can be among other sources of internal distractions. In addition, failing to eat sensibly or get enough sleep can be a powerful distraction because, after a while, you won't have enough energy to concentrate fully in your classes or on your outside assignments. If this is the case, you need to stop cheating yourself.

There's yet another internal distraction that sometimes makes it difficult for college freshmen to concentrate. This distraction is the loss of perspective that can result from having to deal with unfamiliar new people and situations. There are many good ways to keep your perspective when faced with those kinds of personal challenges. Here are four suggestions that can help.

- *Don't worry about the small stuff.* Don't make a big issue out of every small inconvenience. Instead, recognize that minor frictions, disappointments, and even failures are part of life and that most frustrations stem from little matters that will take care of themselves in good time.

- *Get away from it once in a while.* Sometimes when things go wrong, it helps to escape from the situation for a while. Don't let your emotions take control. Get away long enough to regain your perspective so you can deal with the problem when you are more composed. It can be quite relaxing to lose yourself in a movie or take a weekend trip. Afterwards, you'll probably find yourself better able to deal with whatever was troubling you.

- *Put yourself in the other person's shoes.* Don't consider only your own side of a question or disagreement. Try to look at the situation from the other person's point of view. Be willing to acknowledge the validity of his or her interpretation. Learning to compromise is easier once you understand and respect each other's positions.

- *Don't bottle up your frustrations.* When something worries you, confide in somebody you can trust. Talking out a problem or worry reduces your anxiety about it because the process helps you to see the matter more objectively and decide how it can be resolved.

4. Learn to Value Time on Your Own

Although cooperative study sometimes is appropriate, don't make the mistake of thinking of studying as a social activity. Much of the time, there's no practical alternative to studying more or less on your own. If you want to study effectively, you must learn to temporarily separate yourself from the rest of the world—if not physically, then at least mentally—and do without human interaction for a while.

For students who find it hard to settle down and study, the solitary nature of studying often is at the root of the problem. One way to overcome the feeling of isolation that you might have when you're studying is to think of your study time as a chance to have some privacy and to think on your own. That's a major part of the college experience—discovering who you are, what you like to do, what you're best at, and where you want to go with your life.

Summary:
Managing Your "Psychological Environment"

1. Build a positive attitude toward your studies by setting goals for yourself and by using self-talk strategies to psych yourself "up" rather than "out."
2. When you study, get right down to business, keep up the pace, and don't allow any of your time or effort to be wasted.
3. Work on improving your study concentration and take action on any situation, external or internal, that reduces your ability to concentrate.
4. Learn to value the time you spend studying alone as an opportunity to grow personally and intellectually.

Wrap-Up

This chapter has taken a close look at some of the most common problems that college freshmen and other students have with managing their study time and environment. It also has presented proven ways of overcoming those problems. The chapter dealt with time and environment separately, but, of course, the two can't really be separated. To manage your time, you must also manage your environment. The opposite is equally true.

You've learned ten time management tips and seen that the key to using your time effectively is putting yourself on a schedule. You've read some suggestions about planning and scheduling your study time and other activities—both for the academic term and for each week of the term. Skill Builders 1 and 2 gave you a chance to practice your new skills in time management. To ensure a successful transition to the academic and social demands of college, keep practicing your skills and monitoring your progress. Adjust your schedule if necessary.

You've also seen that there's more to your study environment than tables, chairs, lamps, and books. In addition to those and other elements of your physical environment, there's your psychological environment. It's probably every bit as important as your physical environment. That's because mental traits such as a positive attitude and good concentration can help you overcome study surroundings or conditions that are less than ideal. You've learned four steps in managing your physical environment and four steps in managing your psychological environment. In Skill Builder 3 you started putting some of these new ideas to work.

Progress Check

This chapter has covered a lot of material. Some of it you may already have known. Probably, though, some of the material was new to you. Take a moment now to look back at the Self-Help Checklist that you completed at the beginning of the chapter. Review any statements for which your answers differed from those in the key. Given what you know now about managing your time and environment, would you respond differently to the statements? More important, are you willing to work on improving any ineffective study skills, habits, or attitudes that might reduce your chances for success in college?

While you're looking back at the checklist, you might want to review the goals that you wrote down earlier. Do you feel that you've made progress toward your goals? If not, don't be discouraged. Developing new skills, habits, and attitudes takes time and practice. Although this chapter is about to end, your progress in managing time and environment is really only beginning.

Use the following blanks to write down either the three most important and useful ideas that you've gained from this chapter or the three time and environment goals that you want to work on next.

IDEA/GOAL 1: ____________________

____

____

____

IDEA/GOAL 2: ____________________

____

____

____

IDEA/GOAL 3: ____________________

____

____

____

Next Steps

It's probably best not to try taking immediate action on *everything* you've learned in this chapter. Work on the matters that are most important to you right now. Then return to this chapter for more ideas as you're ready for them. Keep practicing your skills in management of time and environment. Keep checking your progress. Managing your time and managing your environment effectively are more than just good study skills to master. They're valuable life skills worth working on every day.

Two of the Skill Builder forms in this chapter—the Daily Activity List and the Weekly Activity Schedule—can help you keep developing your new skills. Extra copies of these forms are provided in Appendix A in the back of this book. You may want to leave one of each form blank so you can make photocopies.

Chapter 2

Reading Textbooks

Warm-Up

How do you feel about textbooks?

If you're like many college students, you may have the same indifferent feelings about your textbooks as about, for instance, your toothpaste and socks. You acknowledge that they're necessary, but you don't get very excited about them.

When you stop to think about it, though, you'll realize that textbooks aren't meant to be exciting. They're meant to inform you. Unlike popular magazines, light novels, and other publications intended as entertainment, textbooks contain little fluff or filler. They are usually solid information from front cover to back cover.

As a college student, you are responsible for learning the information in your textbooks and demonstrating your knowledge on examinations. To do so effectively, you have to approach textbook reading quite differently from the way you approach reading for entertainment, relaxation, or escape. Also, because the volume of assigned reading is so much greater in college than in high school, you'll probably have to alter the reading habits and techniques that you used for your high school classes. This chapter will show you how it's done.

Overview and Benefits

This chapter offers an in-depth look at the main features of textbook organization. It also provides eight tips for keeping pace with your assigned readings, getting more information out of your textbooks, and retaining and recalling your knowledge more effectively. Skill Builder 4 will give you a chance to start using these tips with one of your own textbooks.

The chapter also covers the five steps of the SQ3R system for mastering textbooks. Skill Builder 5 will give you some practice in applying SQ3R to a sample of textbook material.

There are at least five major ways that improved textbook reading skills can help you in college and in your future activities.

- You'll increase your ability to concentrate on written material and to understand and remember what you are reading.
- You'll get more out of lectures and class discussions that are based on, or related to, your reading assignments.
- You'll find it easier to get ready for tests and major exams. With time and practice, you should improve your grades.
- If you're going on to get more education or training after your undergraduate work, you'll be prepared for the increased amount and complexity of required reading.
- You'll be better able to handle the informational reading that will be necessary to keep up to date in your future job.

Checking Your Present Skills

The Self-Help Checklist on the next page can help you to start analyzing your present skills, habits, and attitudes related to reading textbooks. Read each of the ten statements carefully and then mark your answer. Circle the letter "T" if the statement is *true* for you. Circle "F" if the statement is *false* for you.

Be honest with yourself. This checklist is for your use only, and no one else need see your answers. Mark the answers that accurately describe your approach to reading textbooks—even if, in some cases, your answers differ from obviously "right" answers. Be sure to respond to all ten statements.

Self-Help Checklist:
Reading Textbooks

---

1. T F I tend to daydream when I'm reading my assignments.

2. T F I skip most review questions and exercises included in a textbook assignment.

3. T F As I read a textbook assignment, I often try to think of likely exam questions about the material.

4. T F I avoid underlining, highlighting, or making notes in my textbooks.

5. T F I don't start reading my textbook assignments until an exam on the material is announced.

6. T F When I read a textbook assignment, I study the illustrations, graphs, or tables included.

7. T F Before I begin reading a textbook assignment, I try to scan the topic headings and subheadings.

8. T F When I don't understand an unfamiliar word in a textbook, I usually look it up in the glossary or a dictionary.

9. T F I find it difficult to keep up with the amount of reading assigned by my instructors.

10. T F When I finish a reading assignment, I try to summarize the main points that were covered.

- Statements 3, 6, 7, 8, and 10 are almost always *true* for students with good skills and habits in textbook reading and positive attitudes about the process.
- Statements 1, 2, 4, 5, and 9 are almost always *false* for students with good skills and habits in textbook reading and positive attitudes about the process.

What Do You Need to Work On?

The statements in the Self-Help Checklist are based on specific skills, habits, and attitudes that present problems for many college students. Look back over your answers to see how they compare with the key below the checklist.

As you do so, reread the ten statements. Ask yourself which of your textbook-related skills, habits, or attitudes you would most like to strengthen. This chapter can help you with all of the matters covered in the checklist—and many more.

How Textbooks Are Organized

Textbooks don't just happen. It takes a year or more of effort by many highly skilled people to plan, research, write, and print a typical college textbook. As a result of the care that goes into them, most textbooks are organized in a logical way. If you know what to look for, the organizational structure of a textbook can help you find your way through the material. That's true no matter how difficult the material is or how dry you consider the assignment.

Knowing the organizational structure of a textbook gives you an advantage when it comes to understanding and learning the information. On the other hand, trying to read a textbook without being aware of its structure is a lot like starting off on a long trip by car without a road map or detailed directions. In either case, you run the risk of getting lost before you reach your destination.

Regardless of the subjects that they deal with, most college textbooks have certain organizational features in common. These features are intended to help you read, understand, and remember the material. Nine such features are discussed in this section. Pick some of your textbooks and look for these features in each of them as you progress through the following pages. Doing this will help you identify standard textbook features more easily in your next reading assignments.

1. Front Matter and Back Matter

Don't assume that the actual textbook chapters are all that you need concern yourself with. At the college level, most textbooks contain a good deal of material that precedes and follows the text chapters. This material, which is often referred to as the *front matter* and *back matter* of a book, is there for a purpose. It helps students gain better understanding of the information in the text. Whether or not your instructors assign the front and back matter in your textbooks, you should know what's there and how to use it.

The *front matter* of a textbook may include any of a dozen or more parts. As you compare the descriptions below with the front matter in your textbooks, note that the pages preceding the main text of a book usually are numbered with small Roman numerals (e.g., i, ii, iii, iv, etc.). The front matter parts likely to be of greatest use to you include the following.

- *Title page.* Gives the full title of the book and (if applicable) the edition number. Also identifies the company that published the book, along with the author(s) and, sometimes, the editor. Often, you'll find not just the names of the author(s) and editor, but also their degrees, academic affiliations, and titles. This information may help you determine whether the people responsible for the content of a book are experts in their field.

- *Copyright page.* Provides the "facts of publication" of a book, including the copyright notice, which establishes legal ownership of the book's content. This page may also offer detailed information on the publishing company, the edition number, and the exact year of printing.

- *Table of contents.* Shows the name or title of each main division of the book and usually the headings and subheadings within these divisions—all with page numbers. The table of contents can serve as a rough guide to the information you'll be expected to learn in a course. You may find it helpful to examine the tables of contents in your textbooks every few weeks. Doing so will make it easier for you to grasp how the topics that you're reading about fit together. If you have an instructor who hasn't distributed a course outline, reviewing the table of contents in your textbook can help you see where the course is going and what topics will be covered along the way.

- *Preface, foreword, introduction, or "To the Reader" page.* Describes, in general terms, the scope and purpose of the book. Sometimes explains the viewpoints of the author(s) and/or editor—for instance, why certain topics are or are not included. May point out any special features of the book that you should be aware of.

The *back matter* of a textbook consists of one or more supplements to the text. Knowing how to use the back matter of a book can help you to understand the text in greater depth. The parts that you're likely to find most useful include the following.

- *Appendix.* Contains material that, while not necessary for basic comprehension of the text, can be of interest to students who would like more information. Documents and other material too lengthy or detailed to be presented in the text (for instance, a series of maps showing German military advances during World War II) sometimes are placed in the appendix of a textbook.
- *Glossary.* An alphabetical list of subject-specific or otherwise uncommon words introduced in the text. For each word, a brief definition is given. When you come upon an unfamiliar word in a reading assignment, underline or highlight it—or write it down in your notebook. The meaning of the word may become clear in the next paragraph. If not, look up the word in the glossary or in a dictionary. Don't rely on guesswork. Understanding key words is essential to learning textbook material.
- *Bibliography.* A list of books and articles related to the topics covered in a textbook. Usually arranged alphabetically by author. A reference list is much like a bibliography but typically includes only those sources that the author(s) used in researching and writing a book. The bibliography or reference list shows where you can look for more information on a particular topic.
- *Index.* An alphabetical list of the main topics and terms in a book. For each major topic, related subtopics are listed below it—again, in alphabetical order. Each entry in an index includes the number(s) of the page or pages where the topic is discussed. The index can be a valuable aid when you're reviewing for an exam and need to find something you read earlier but can't locate by browsing.

2. Text Sections and Chapters

A typical college textbook covers a broad subject in great depth and detail. To help students learn the material, textbooks present their subject matter in a series of ever-smaller divisions. In some textbooks, the first and largest division is the section or "part." Every major topic covered by this kind of textbook usually is presented in a separate section or part, each made up of several chapters.

Even in textbooks that have sections or parts, chapters often are the handiest division of content. Instructors frequently assign readings and exams in terms of the chapters to be covered. This is a logical way to work with the content of a textbook. The larger sections or parts may each cover several hundred pages. Chapters typically are shorter—often only 25 to 50 pages.

A textbook chapter usually is divided into a number of discussions, each dealing with a related subtopic. In other words, a textbook chapter—like the book as a whole—is organized in a way that allows students to master a large body of information in a series of small, manageable steps. If you tend to daydream or get bored during a reading assignment, you can use the chapter's subtopics as short-term goal points. Focus your effort on reading and understanding each subtopic, one at a time, without loss of attention.

3. Introductions and Summaries

Textbook chapters almost always begin with an introduction or overview. Usually no more than one or two paragraphs, the introduction prepares you for learning the material ahead by briefly stating the main points that will be covered.

Textbook chapters usually end with a short summary of the main points. By giving you a quick review, the summary reinforces your knowledge of the material you've read and helps you to remember it more clearly. In some textbooks, the chapters end with review questions or exercises. These function much like a summary, but get you more actively involved in reviewing the material and checking your understanding of it. Review questions and exercises are less common in college texts than in high school texts.

4. Titles and Topic Headings

Each chapter of a textbook has a title that describes, or at least suggests, what the chapter is about. The main topics of the chapter are presented in separate passages of text, each with its own heading. Many textbooks divide the subject matter within topics into subtopics. Subtopics often have their own subheadings.

In most textbooks, each "level" of content has a different type size or type style for its topic headings and subheadings. It's important to be aware of the different levels of headings and subheadings in a given textbook. The headings and subheadings often provide an outline of the book's content. While it's rarely a *perfect* outline, the headings and subheadings can make it much easier for you to see how the topics and subtopics relate to each other. Headings and subheadings also can help you to identify likely exam questions and to think of practice questions for review.

5. Paragraphs and Topic Sentences

Paragraphs and sentences are the smallest divisions of content. Textbook authors often try to begin each paragraph with a topic sentence. The topic sentence of a paragraph serves the same purpose as the introduction of a chapter. It states the main idea of the material that follows it. The rest of the paragraph provides the details, examples, or additional information necessary to develop the idea.

Sometimes, you may find paragraphs that don't begin with topic sentences. When this happens, look elsewhere in the paragraph for the topic sentence. It might be located in the middle of the paragraph, or at the end. Almost every paragraph will have—somewhere in it—a sentence that functions as the key to comprehension. When you make an effort to find and understand the topic sentence, it becomes much easier to learn the main idea of a paragraph.

6. Signal Words and Phrases

Textbooks make generous use of signal words and phrases to help students note main points, connections and transitions, similarities and differences, and fine shades of meaning. There are three kinds of signal words and phrases—introductory, relational, and conclusive. Each of your textbooks probably uses all three kinds of signals.

- *Introductory signals.* These tell you that a point is about to be made or that a body of related, important, and probably detailed information follows. Phrases like "The chief cause," "The three major factors," and "Historically, the five underlying conditions" are introductory signals.
- *Relational signals.* These include a wide variety of words and phrases that can help you follow the connections, transitions, similarities, and differences among the ideas presented in a text. Signals like "First . . . , Second . . . , Third . . ." call your attention to a series of related steps, facts, or concepts. Such words and phrases as "In addition," "Moreover," and "Furthermore" show you that a topic is being continued or expanded. "Likewise" and "By the same token" can mark either the continuation or expansion of a topic or the drawing of a similarity or parallel. "However," "Nevertheless," "Conversely," and "On the other hand" mark exceptions, qualifications, and differences.
- *Conclusive signals.* These resemble some of the relational signals in that they often highlight cause-and-effect relationships. Conclusive signals also serve to let you know that a result, conclusion, or summary is about to be presented. Words and phrases like "Thus," "Therefore," "Consequently," and "In the final analysis" are conclusive signals.

7. Visual Aids

Almost every textbook uses visual aids to reinforce the information in the text. Common types of visual aids include photographs, cartoons, diagrams and other drawings, maps, graphs, charts, and tables.

Most of the time, visual aids are *neither* a substitute for the text *nor* an optional extra that you can safely skip when you're in a hurry. They are usually a vital supplement to the text and should be studied along with it. Three paragraphs of biology text, for instance, can give you an idea of what an amoeba is and how it functions. Studying the diagram, though, allows you to form a mental picture of an amoeba.

8. Lists

Lists are another important feature of many textbooks. Sometimes lists are:

1. set off
2. with numbers
3. like this.

Lists also can be:

- set off
- with "bullets"
- like this.

When you come upon a list in a textbook, you know that the listed material is *related* in some way. For example, a list might be used to present three distinguishing characteristics of mammals or four causes of U.S. military involvement in Southeast Asia.

While it's important to remember each item in such a list, it's equally important to understand how the items fit together to form a logical whole. With some lists, you may need to remember the exact order of the items.

9. Typographical Emphasis

When textbook authors introduce a new word, phrase, or concept—or want you to remember an important point—they often use typographical emphasis to make the material stand out. In some textbooks, *italic type* is used for emphasis. Other textbooks use **boldface type** for the same purpose.

Either way, the typographical emphasis means that you should take particular note of the new material being introduced or the point being made.

Summary:
How Textbooks Are Organized

1. Front matter and back matter

2. Text sections and chapters

3. Introductions and summaries

4. Titles and topic headings

5. Paragraphs and topic sentences

6. Signal words and phrases

7. Visual aids

8. Lists

9. Typographical emphasis

Eight Tips for Mastering College Textbooks

In the previous section, you learned how college textbooks are organized. This section presents eight tips for mastering textbook information and adjusting to the large amount of reading expected of college students. Several of these tips will build on your knowledge of textbook organization. They'll show you how to use organizational features to better understand, remember, and recall your reading assignments.

Because of the great volume of required reading in college, it's essential for students to know and use proven reading techniques. It's especially important for freshmen and for students returning to college after some time away. These students often feel overwhelmed and discouraged by the amount of reading that their instructors assign. For "new" students in this situation, learning how to handle reading assignments effectively is one of the keys to surviving the first year on campus. Whatever *your* situation, the following pointers can help.

1. Read and Review in a Timely Manner

A typical college course is planned so that each reading assignment will prepare students for lecture or discussion in the next meeting of the course. That's probably the way things were for you in high school. College instructors, however, rarely go over a reading assignment in class as painstakingly as high school teachers do. Instead, most college instructors assume that you have read the assigned material and achieved a good basic understanding of it on your own. They use the following class session to build on the text with information from other sources, sometimes including their own study and research.

It stands to reason, then, that to succeed in college you must keep up with your textbook assignments and read each one carefully before the next class session in that course. As you read an assignment, try to formulate some questions of special interest to you. Because the textbook will have given you the basic knowledge you need, you'll go to class prepared to master the new information presented.

Chances are, you'll notice that you're more interested in what's going on in class when you're well prepared. You'll probably notice, too, that you're paying closer attention and that you're listening *actively*—searching for answers to the questions raised by your reading. As a result, your classes will seem less anonymous, more personal, and more relevant. In lectures, you'll find it easier to take good, organized notes for use later in preparing for exams. In labs and discussion classes, you'll become more involved with the activities or questions presented. You may feel more comfortable about speaking up with questions or comments of your own.

Be sure to *review* each reading assignment—and the related class notes—as soon after class as possible. By providing you with a third exposure to the subject matter, regular review of your reading assignments and class notes greatly increases your understanding of the main concepts and the ways that they tie in with each other. If there are gaps in your knowledge of the material, you'll detect them by reviewing and will be able to take action. In addition, regular review improves your retention of the material and pays off later by reducing the amount of time and effort you'll spend in preparing for midterms and finals.

2. Integrate New Material as You Read It

Reading, understanding, and remembering the information in your textbook assignments is only part of learning the material. An equally important step is integrating new textbook material, as you read it, with what you've learned previously. In other words, you must make sure that new information connects logically with what you already know about the subject.

A good way of integrating new learning with old is to briefly review your *previous* reading assignment in a subject before starting a new reading assignment. Then, as you read, look for connections between the new material and what you've already learned. Another good idea is to frequently compare your reading assignments with your class notes. In this way, you'll see how textbook information complements information gathered in lectures, class discussions, and labs to round out your understanding of a given topic.

Now and then, you may want to write out brief summary notes, in outline form, to unify the information from all sources on a topic. At a minimum, try to regularly cross-reference your class notes with your textbook readings. You can do this by adding textbook references in the margins of your notes whenever it seems helpful to do so. For instance, you might write, "Chapt. 13 has historical background" or "See Fuller, pp. 212-227, for different interpretation." By integrating new information as you learn it, you'll acquire in-depth knowledge of your course material rather than mere familiarity with some loosely connected facts.

3. Read Actively

Because they're packed with information, college textbooks require a reading style quite different from the casual style you might use for recreational reading. Textbooks require *active* reading. Active reading is study reading, reading geared toward understanding and remembering the material. A simple but effective active reading strategy is to mentally convert textbook headings and subheadings into Who, What, When, Where, Why, and How questions. Then, as you read the assignment, challenge yourself to answer each of the questions. Skill Builder 4 will give you some practice in converting textbook headings into questions.

Perhaps the best active reading strategy—when it's done properly—is underlining or highlighting key portions of text. Many college freshmen, however, have trouble with underlining or highlighting text. This is understandable. High school students usually don't own their books and aren't allowed to mark in them. As a result of their lack of experience, some freshmen tend to overdo it when they mark their textbooks. Too much underlining or highlighting defeats the intended purpose of the markings, which is to make the *essentials* stand out for easy identification during review. In fact, excessive textbook marking is worse than none at all.

Train yourself to mark your textbooks with restraint. Even with very dense, difficult texts, probably no more than 10% to 15% of the material should be underlined or highlighted. You'll find it easier to limit your markings if you read an entire paragraph, or series of paragraphs, before making any marks. Marking *as* you read almost always leads to excess. Try to mark only the key words and phrases. In effect, you're making an outline for later review when you mark a text. Your outline will be useful, though, only if it's brief and uncluttered.

Don't underline or highlight entire paragraphs. Ideally, you shouldn't even mark entire sentences. If a whole sentence or paragraph seems important, just place a bracket beside it in the outside margin of the page. If there's a word or phrase that serves as a key to the bracketed sentence or paragraph, underline or highlight only the key material. You could also write the key words and phrases in the margin. Never mark in library books or other publications that don't belong to you.

Careful marking of your textbooks can help to keep you alert when you're reading. That's because, in order to underline or highlight properly, you must concentrate on the material and evaluate everything you read so you'll know what's worth marking. An added benefit of careful textbook marking will become apparent when it's time for midterms and finals. If you had to review 450 pages of reading for an exam, which of the following would you rather work with?

- Unmarked text?
- Excessively marked text?
- "Cleanly" marked text in which the underlined or highlighted words and phrases make up a concise outline of the material?

4. Read Flexibly

Closely related to the skill of reading actively is the skill of reading flexibly. Flexible reading means adjusting your reading speed and intensity according to a number of factors. These factors include the difficulty of the material and your background and ability in the subject area. For instance, you might need to spend as much time and effort on three pages of physics text covering an unfamiliar, complex principle or theory as you would on ten to 20 pages of history text covering a topic or period that you already know something about.

Don't be overly concerned about building up your reading speed. Unless you are vision-impaired or have a learning disability that severely limits your reading speed, you probably read fast enough at present. In fact, if you're like many freshmen, you may be reading your textbooks *too* fast. Don't assume that you can or should breeze through your textbook assignments in college the way that you may have in high school.

If you're finding that you read just a little too slowly to keep up with the amount of material you have to cover, don't be discouraged. The next section of this chapter will introduce you to SQ3R, an organized strategy for textbook reading. With SQ3R, you can gradually increase both your reading comprehension *and* your speed.

Learn to adjust your reading speed and intensity to the nature of the task. When you find the text difficult, slow down, bear down, and make sure you're really learning the material. In places, it may be necessary to reread a sentence or an entire paragraph that's unclear to you. Where the text is less difficult, you can probably afford to pick up the pace.

5. Read Critically

All textbooks try to give balanced, objective presentations of the topics that they deal with. However, no textbook can possibly present all views on a given topic, nor can any textbook be regarded as the ultimate authority on a topic. For this reason, you must read your textbooks in a critical frame of mind. You should evaluate what you read and, within reasonable limits, draw your own conclusions.

Be careful, though. Critical reading doesn't mean that you can skip over textbook material that you disagree with. Before you can disagree with a textbook passage or judge it in any way, you must first read it closely and understand it.

Critical reading means applying higher-level reading skills such as comparing different viewpoints and consulting a variety of information sources to arrive at your own balanced view of a topic or issue. Related skills include identifying the author's biases, determining his or her qualifications, distinguishing facts from opinions, and sorting out main points from minor details. In short, critical reading is intelligent reading—a skill that can serve you well for your entire adult life.

6. Test Your Understanding as You Read

One of the keys to mastering your textbooks is to test your understanding of the material as you read. Make it a habit to quiz yourself at short intervals in your reading assignments. For instance, after each series of related paragraphs, stop and ask yourself questions like these.

- What is the central focus or "message" of the material?
- What are the main points or concepts presented?
- How do they add to and tie in with prior material on the subject?

Answer these questions in your own words, without looking at the text. If you can't answer such basic questions, then you haven't really learned the material. You'll have to go back and reread or review before you move on. Make it a rule never to leave a passage of text until you fully understand what you've just read.

Another way to test your understanding is to take turns summarizing material with a classmate. In Chapter 1, Managing Time and Environment, you saw that cooperative study (studying with a partner) can be a good way to review for an exam. Another situation in which cooperative study can prove helpful is when you have to read and understand a difficult textbook assignment. Handling that task cooperatively could involve the following steps.

1. Both students silently read the same portion of the assigned text.
2. While one student listens, the other recalls aloud the main points of the passage.
3. The listener notes any errors or omissions and offers additional thoughts as appropriate. Either student asks questions about material not fully understood.
4. Both students silently read the next portion of text and then reverse roles.

7. Study the Visual Aids

As you learned earlier in this chapter, visual aids—like tables, graphs, diagrams, and maps—are an important part of textbooks. Visual aids increase your understanding of a topic by *showing* you information that might have required hundreds of words of text to explain. No matter what form they take, most visual aids expand and reinforce your understanding of the text by making abstract concepts, and the relationships among them, concrete.

In reading a textbook assignment, be sure to examine all visual aids included and study those that convey solid information. A good first step is to quickly scan a visual aid to determine whether it's truly informative. Although the practice is much less common in college texts than in high school texts, visual aids sometimes are used just to fill out a "short" page or to break up a long, dense stretch of text. Waste no time or effort on visual aids of that kind.

When you've determined that a visual aid *does* have information value, read its heading or caption to see what topic it deals with. Then, look over the visual aid as a whole to familiarize yourself with its parts or features. Next, read any explanatory material beneath or beside the visual aid—for example, a footnote to a table, or the key or legend of a map.

Then study the displayed information itself. Read all subheadings, labels, or other identifiers so you'll understand exactly what is being shown. Whenever a visual aid presents numerical data, make sure you know what the units of measurement are. When you've taken all of these steps, check your mastery of the visual aid by seeing whether you can express its main points in a few sentences.

8. Go Beyond the Text When Necessary

While textbooks rarely contain factual errors, they sometimes present complex or controversial topics in a simplified way. For some students, that kind of textbook presentation may be *over*simplified and seem incomplete, ambiguous, or even contradictory.

If a textbook ever leaves you with unanswered questions, there are three things you should do. First, give yourself a pat on the back for reading actively and critically. Second, don't assume that your knowledge of a topic has to be limited to what's in the textbook. Third, write down your question and go beyond the textbook to get the information you need.

There are several ways of going beyond the textbook. The most obvious are to take part in class discussions and, if appropriate, to ask questions during or after lectures. Unless a student is just showing off, college instructors almost always welcome questions and comments that help to broaden the class's knowledge beyond the information in the textbook. Chances are, the responses of your classmates and instructor will help you resolve your unanswered questions. If not, ask your instructor to recommend a book or journal article on the topic.

You could also research the topic yourself, using the resources of the campus library. (As you'll learn in Chapter 4, Using Information Resources, there are very few questions that can't be answered when you know your way around your college library.) By going beyond the information in your textbooks, you may develop an interest that results in some original ideas for a research paper or similar project. You may even discover an interest strong enough to suggest directions for your future course work or career.

Summary:
Eight Tips for Mastering College Textbooks

1. Do your reading assignments before the material is lectured on or discussed in class. Review them as soon after class as possible.

2. With each textbook assignment, make an effort to integrate the new material with what you've learned in your previous readings and class discussions.

3. Read actively and make careful use of underlining or highlighting to simplify later review for exams.

4. Read flexibly, adjusting your speed and intensity to the difficulty of the material and to your ability.

5. Read critically, to identify authors' biases and to distinguish facts from opinions.

6. Test your understanding of textbook material by frequently asking yourself questions as you read. Answer your questions by restating the main points of the assignment in your own words.

7. Study informative visual aids along with the text to increase your understanding of the topics covered.

8. Develop ways of going beyond the text when necessary to clear up uncertainties or to get more information about a topic.

Skill Builder 4:
Changing Headings Into Questions

This Skill Builder will give you a chance to see for yourself that turning textbook headings into questions—and then reading actively to find the answers—really can improve your mastery of textbook material.

INSTRUCTIONS

- In a textbook for one of your courses, pick a short chapter or passage of text that you haven't yet read. Using the blanks at the top of the Textbook Headings Worksheet on the next page, write down the name of the course, the title of the textbook, and the title of the chapter you've picked.
- Write the first heading of the chapter in the blank marked "Heading 1." Then mentally convert the heading into the kind of Who, What, When, Where, Why, or How question that a good investigative reporter would ask in researching an article on the topic of the heading. Write your question in the blank provided.
- Read all of the textbook material under the first heading. As you do so, challenge yourself to find the answer to your question. Write the answer, in your own words, in the blanks provided. If you read the material carefully and make an effort to really understand its meaning, you'll probably find that you can sum up many lines of text in just a few well chosen words of your own.
- Using other headings in the chapter, repeat this series of steps for the four remaining sets of blanks on the worksheet. Try to make each of your questions more to the point than the one before. In your answers, try to express the maximum amount of information in the fewest words possible.

Textbook Headings Worksheet

Name of Course: ______________________

Textbook Title: ______________________

Chapter Title: ______________________
(or page numbers of passage)

Heading 1: ______________________

Question: ______________________

Answer: ______________________

____

____

Heading 2: ______________________

Question: ______________________

Answer: ______________________

____

____

Heading 3: ______________________

Question: ______________________

Answer: ______________________

____

____

Heading 4: ______________________

Question: ______________________

Answer: ______________________

____

____

Heading 5: ______________________

Question: ______________________

Answer: ______________________

____

____

SQ3R—The Reading Method That Really Works

Francis P. Robinson was an Ohio State University professor who specialized in educational research. Through his research, he developed many ideas to help students study and learn more effectively. One of Robinson's research interests was reading. His experience as a researcher and college professor had convinced him that most students—even very good ones—have difficulty reading, understanding, and remembering the information in their textbooks. The reason, he found, is that few students have an *organized strategy* for textbook reading.

Robinson developed an easy-to-learn, five-step strategy for reading textbooks. He called this strategy the SQ3R Reading Method. The *S*, the *Q*, and the three *R*s stand for the five steps in the method—Survey, Question, Read, Recite, Review.

Millions of students in colleges and high schools have used SQ3R to get more meaning out of their textbooks with less difficulty. SQ3R also makes it easier to review for exams and, with practice, can help students of all abilities increase their reading speed and perhaps earn higher grades.

There are four ways in which SQ3R can help *you* right now.

- You'll concentrate better on your textbook assignments.
- You'll learn textbook material more thoroughly and understand it in greater depth and detail.
- You'll get a clearer picture of the connections among the major ideas in a reading assignment, and of the ways that they're developed and supported with minor points.
- You'll remember textbook material longer and recall it more effectively on exams.

Learning and Applying SQ3R

The five steps of the SQ3R Reading Method are explained on the following pages. Like any other new skill, learning SQ3R will require time, effort, and frequent practice on your part. While you're learning the method, you may find that your reading assignments take *more* time rather than less. Stick with it, though. The earlier sections on textbook organization and reading tips have prepared you for success with SQ3R.

When you're just starting to learn the method, apply the five steps to *short* sections of text—for instance, two or three pages covering a single topic. As you become more skilled at using SQ3R and gain confidence in its power to help you master college textbook material, gradually extend your range to cover more pages at one sitting. In Skill Builder 5, you'll have a chance to use SQ3R on one or more short samples of text.

If an instructor recommends a different reading method for his or her course, by all means give that method a try. First, though, learn SQ3R and use it regularly as your front-line reading strategy. It's the basis for many other reading methods and works well with textbooks in a wide variety of subject areas.

1. Survey

First, before you begin to read a textbook assignment, take three to five minutes to *survey* the material and find out what it's about. Read the introduction and summary. They highlight the main ideas you'll have to learn when you read the full assignment. They also point out the connections you'll need to look for among the concepts presented.

Read the topic headings and subheadings, too. As you saw earlier, these often form a rough outline of the material. At the very least, they'll *suggest* how the information is going to be divided up and presented to you. If you pay attention to the headings and subheadings in your textbooks, you'll find it much easier to follow the relationships among topics. Be sure to preview all visual aids to get a sense of how they will reinforce the ideas in the text.

2. Question

Second, sharpen your curiosity about the material by asking yourself a general *question*: "What are the main points that the author is trying to make?" Then convert the topic headings and subheadings into the kind of Who, What, When, Where, Why, and How questions that you practiced in Skill Builder 4. Challenge yourself to dig out the answers as you read. Doing so will maintain your interest and concentration by personalizing the learning task for you. This procedure will also help you to identify and prepare for many of the questions that could be asked about the material on an exam.

3. Read

Third, *read* the assignment carefully for meaning. Read actively, flexibly, and critically, using your knowledge of signal words and phrases to help you follow what the author is saying. Make sure not to overlook any of the headings, subheadings, or visual aids. Answer the questions that you've made from the topic headings. Adjust your reading speed and intensity to the difficulty of the material. When necessary, back up and reread a tough sentence or paragraph. Sort out the facts from the author's opinions, and the main concepts from the supporting details and examples. Think about how the information fits in with, and adds to, what you've learned previously.

To assist in learning, retention, and later review of the information, carefully mark the text (if you own the book) as described in the earlier section on reading tips. Underline or highlight important words and phrases, including definitions, formulas, facts, and concepts. Mark anything that sums up the central meaning of the material, but remember to exercise restraint. Try not to mark more than 10% to 15% of what you read. Don't make a practice of underlining or highlighting whole sentences. If a sentence or paragraph seems *that* important, bracket the material in the outside margin of the page. You may want to put a star or other eye-catching symbol in the margin beside any information that you think might make a good exam question.

4. Recite

Fourth, whenever the text shifts from one topic or subtopic to another, stop and *recite* to yourself the main points covered. Reciting means restating the main points in your own words, without looking at the text. Afterward, check yourself against the text to make sure that you've understood it. If you haven't restated the main points correctly and completely, you haven't really learned the material. Go back and reread or skim the sections that you're uncertain about. Then try reciting again.

Reciting from memory is one of the best ways to make sure that you're learning and retaining textbook information. Like the cooperative study procedure described earlier in this chapter, reciting to yourself immediately reveals any gaps in your knowledge of the material and gives you an opportunity to remedy them on the spot. Reciting also provides you with practice in answering the kinds of questions that eventually will appear on an exam. If you feel that reciting isn't worth the bother, ask yourself this: "If I can't restate the main points of a textbook assignment as I read it, what will my chances be when I'm questioned about the material on an exam?"

5. Review

Finally, *review* the reading assignment to perfect your understanding and retention of the material. Reviewing is the process of actively going over information you've studied to fix it clearly in your memory. Don't put off reviewing until just before an exam. That's a good time for your final, brush-up review, but not for your first review. Research has shown that the best time for a first review of textbook material is right after you've read it.

In reviewing, look back over the *entire* reading assignment, including the topic headings and subheadings and the key words and phrases that you marked. Concentrate hardest on the *main concepts,* especially any that you had trouble with on first reading and any that you've identified as possible exam questions. In places, you might find it necessary to back up to steps 3 and 4 for rereading and re-reciting difficult material. The goal is never to close your book on a reading assignment until you're certain that you have complete mastery and recall of the key information.

Summary:
SQ3R—The Reading Method That Really Works

1. **Survey** each textbook assignment before you begin reading it. Skim the introduction and summary, the topic headings and subheadings, and the visual aids. This will familiarize you with the concepts you'll be expected to learn.

2. **Question** yourself about the main points to be covered in the assignment. Turn the headings and subheadings into Who, What, When, Where, Why, and How questions to be answered as you read.

3. **Read** the assignment actively, flexibly, and critically to answer the questions that you've posed. To simplify reviewing for exams, carefully underline or highlight key words and phrases that sum up the essentials of the material.

4. **Recite** the main points of the assignment from memory, in your own words. Then check yourself against the text to make sure that you've learned the material and will be able to recall it later on an exam.

5. **Review** the entire reading assignment and put extra effort on any section or topic that you're not fully confident about. Repeat steps 3 and 4 if necessary to master the material and fix it firmly in your memory.

Skill Builder 5:
Using SQ3R

In this Skill Builder, you'll practice using the SQ3R Reading Method and marking key words and phrases in one or more short selections of text.

INSTRUCTIONS

- Quickly examine the three samples of textbook material on the following pages. Note that the samples represent different kinds of subject matter and different degrees of difficulty.
- Applying the five steps of the SQ3R Reading Method, read one or more of the samples of textbook material. Before starting to read the material, you may want to briefly review the SQ3R summary on the previous page.
- As you read the textbook material, carefully mark the text as though you were preparing it for later review. Try to underline or highlight only the words and phrases that are *essential* for comprehension of the material. When you're finished, compare your markings with those in the answer key in Appendix B.

PASSAGE #1

LANDING A SMALL AIRPLANE

A pilot must follow a strict sequence of three steps in landing a small plane. These three steps, though simple enough in themselves, must always occur in the correct order.

Turn on the Carburetor Heat

The first step is to turn on the carburetor heat. This is essential because the next step, pulling back on the throttle, could otherwise cause freezing in the carburetor, which could cause a complete loss of power. Thus, turning on the carburetor heat is a very important first step.

Pull Back on the Throttle

The pilot then pulls back on the throttle and raises the nose of the plane. This reduces the airspeed, which must be done before taking the next step, lowering the flaps on the wings. Failure to reduce the airspeed before lowering the flaps could cause enough stress on the wings to result in structural damage. Needless to say, any structural damage to the wings is potentially dangerous.

Lower the Flaps

After reducing the airspeed, the pilot lowers the flaps. This makes it possible for the plane to sustain flight at a lower airspeed, which makes landing safer.

PASSAGE #2

REFRIGERATION

Characteristics of a Gas

Temperature changes often accompany the compression or expansion of a gas. Modern refrigeration is made possible as a result of these changes.

Compression Increases Temperature

In the case of compression, the temperatures of most gases increase. Under some circumstances, the temperature change can be large enough to initiate a chemical reaction. One effective demonstration of this is the "fire stick," a tube with a hand plunger for compressing the air. If a wisp of cotton is placed in the bottom of the tube and the air is rapidly compressed, the cotton will burn with a flash. The same effect is responsible for the operation of the diesel engine, which, unlike the gasoline engine, does not have a spark plug to trigger combustion when the engine is running.

Expansion Decreases Temperature

If a compressed gas is allowed to expand, the opposite effect results; the temperature of the gas decreases. On a small scale, this occurs when air is released from a tire. On a larger scale, it occurs when a mass of air rises; as the mass of air ascends, it expands because the surrounding pressure decreases. The consequent temperature drop may be so large that the moisture in the air condenses to form a cloud.

Use of Gas in Refrigeration

Both compression and expansion principles are used in the design of the refrigerator. In a refrigerator, a gas circulates in a closed loop that includes a compressor (placed outside the refrigerator to compress the gas) and 2 sets of coils for heat transfer (1 inside and 1 outside the refrigerator). If a compressed gas is allowed to expand immediately, it simply cools to its original temperature. However, if the warm gas is first allowed to cool somewhat (by passing it through the coils outside the refrigerator), any subsequent expansion of the gas results in a gas at a temperature lower than the original temperature.

A substance that remains in the gaseous phase throughout this compression-expansion cycle transfers only a small amount of heat in each cycle. Considerably more heat is released when a gas is compressed to a liquid than when a gas is compressed to a denser gas. Thus the refrigeration process is made efficient by using a gas that condenses to a liquid when it is compressed; a large amount of heat is therefore released in each cycle of refrigerator operation.

PASSAGE #3

GROSS NATIONAL PRODUCT: A KEY ECONOMIC INDICATOR

One widely used indicator of the nation's yearly economic performance is **Gross National Product,** or **GNP.** To understand the importance of GNP as an economic indicator, it is necessary to examine what GNP measures and how it reflects the status of the major sectors of the economy.

The Scope of GNP

Gross National Product measures the total dollar value of all final **goods** (for example, a loaf of bread or a television) and **services** (for example, a haircut or a medical check-up) produced in America during a given year. Calculated and announced annually by the U.S. Department of Commerce, GNP is expressed in numbers so large as to be meaningful only to trained economists and statisticians. In recent years, GNP volume has grown into the trillions of dollars.

It should be noted that the Commerce Department includes in GNP only the value of **final** goods and services. **Intermediate** goods and services (those used in the production of final goods and services) are not counted in the GNP calculation. The reason for this distinction is that the value of final goods and services includes the value of all intermediate goods and services used in their production. Thus, for example, the value of a loaf of bread (a final good) would be counted in GNP, but the value of the flour and other ingredients (intermediate goods) used in making it would not be counted.

The Components of GNP

One way of calculating GNP is to add up expenditures for final goods and services that were produced in the U.S. during the year. In calculating GNP by this method, the Commerce Department analyzes the expenditures of the four sectors of the economy that buy goods and services: **private consumers, business and industry, government,** and **foreign interests.** From year to year, each of these groups adjusts its purchasing behavior in response to the actual or expected economic conditions that it is subject to, producing positive or negative effects on GNP.

Expenditures by Private Consumers

Private consumers, both households and individuals, make up the largest of the four sectors of the economy, and their expenditures constitute the largest component of GNP. The personal consumption of households and individuals accounts for almost two-thirds of all goods and services purchased. Private consumers allocate their purchases according to their personal financial circumstances and the state of the economy.

For example, when their incomes rise, consumers tend to buy relatively more **durable goods,** such as cars and washing machines, rather than **nondurable goods,** such as clothing and groceries. Compared to the other components of GNP, the overall level of consumer spending is more stable from year to year.

Expenditures by Business and Industry

The expenditures of business and industry make up the most volatile component of GNP. This is because, while consumers must spend money on basic necessities like food, clothing, and housing regardless of income levels or prices, the business sector of the economy has the option of postponing the construction of a new factory or the purchase of new machinery when economic conditions are unfavorable. Typically, businesses invest in expansion or improvements when they expect the economy to perform well and defer such investment when they expect the economy to be sluggish.

Expenditures by Government

A third component of GNP is government expenditures. The kinds of goods and services purchased vary considerably at each of the three levels of the government sector of the economy: **federal, state,** and **local.** For example, state and local governments spend proportionately more on the education of their citizens than does the federal government. Indeed, for some state and local governments, education is the single most expensive item in their budgets. A continued decline in the number of school-aged children might slow the growth of expenditures for education and thus reduce the positive impact on GNP of state and local government spending.

Expenditures by Foreign Interests

The fourth component of GNP is the expenditures of the various foreign interests that purchase American goods and services. The foreign-based sector of the economy includes both governments and business and industry. Foreign purchases tend to center most heavily on high-technology items, such as electronic communications equipment and military weapons systems, and basic foodstuffs, such as wheat and other grains. Gross national product is positively affected when the United States sells more to foreign interests than it buys from them.

Wrap-Up

This chapter has presented information about how to read, understand, remember, and recall textbook material more effectively. In the first part of the chapter, you saw that textbooks have an orderly structure intended to help students master the content in a series of small steps. You learned nine features of textbook organization, from front matter, back matter, and text to visual aids, lists, and typographical emphasis.

You also studied eight tips for mastering college texts and keeping up with textbook assignments. The tips included such strategies as reading actively, flexibly, and critically. Skill Builder 4 gave you a chance to apply an active reading technique—turning textbook headings into questions and reading to find the answers.

You then learned about the five steps of the SQ3R Reading Method. In Skill Builder 5, you started putting SQ3R to work on sample textbook material. You also practiced marking key words and phrases to simplify reviewing for exams.

Progress Check

This chapter has covered a lot of material. You may already have been familiar with some of the information. Probably, though, much of it was new to you. Here's a chance to find out what you've learned.

Take a few moments now to answer the eight questions that follow. Try to answer them from memory, and in your own words. If you can't remember every detail, it's all right to look back through the chapter. When you've finished, check your work against the key in Appendix B.

1. List three of the signal words and phrases that textbook authors use to help students follow the information being presented. Briefly explain what each of your choices means.

■ ____

____

■ ____

____

■ ____

____

2. What are the two kinds of typographical emphasis most commonly used in textbooks to make a key point stand out or to introduce a new word or concept?

■ ____

■ ____

3. Name four kinds of visual aids that are often used in textbooks.

■ ____

■ ____

■ ____

■ ____

4. What are three of the parts or features that may be included in the back matter of a textbook?

- appendix
- index bibliography
- glossary

5. State two ways of clarifying or going beyond the information in a textbook.

- participate class discussion
- ask questions during/after lecture

6. What are the five steps, in order, of the SQ3R Reading Method?

- survey
- question
- read
- recite
- review

7. Name three of the one-word questions that can help you in turning textbook headings into questions.

- who when
- what how
- where

8. What does the word "recite" mean to you?

- say aloud to yourself — what you have learned from memory. - restating main points of text without looking at text.

Next Steps

The improvement of your skills in reading textbooks shouldn't stop with the end of this chapter. In fact, this is really just the beginning of your improvement. If you're willing to work at it, you can master higher-level reading skills that will benefit you throughout the rest of your college years, in any further education or training you undertake after graduation, and in your future employment.

Practice strengthening those reading skills that are most important to you right now—the ones that you feel could make the difference between failure, survival, and real success in college. Don't set yourself up for disappointment by expecting too much progress too fast. Instead, give yourself a realistic goal of steady, gradual improvement in a *few* important skill areas. You can always return to this chapter for more ideas as you're ready for them.

Apply your new skills in all of your courses. Although your overall textbook reading skills are bound to improve with effort and practice, you may find that progress comes more slowly in some courses than in others. If you have difficulty with the textbook for a particular course, see your instructor. He or she may be able to recommend specialized reading strategies tailored to the subject area. If you think that you need additional help, check with the people at your campus reading lab, study skills center, or academic advising center.

Chapter 3

Taking Class Notes

Warm-Up

Almost every college student has a notebook of some sort and takes it to class. Almost every student opens his or her notebook in class, gets out a pen or pencil, and jots a few notes on the lecture. Here, though, the similarities end. Well prepared students take complete, organized notes on all of the main ideas and supporting details presented in class. Other students record only a few dates, facts, formulas, definitions, or examples and generally fail to write down, or clearly understand, the context and meaning of the information.

Many students who don't take organized notes would like to do better but lack an effective note taking procedure. They don't know what to record, or how. Some find it hard to keep up with the rapid-fire lecturer often encountered in large, introductory courses. And a few such students simply don't realize the importance of taking good notes in class. "Why bother?" they reason. "I'll remember this. Anyway, it's all in the textbook, isn't it?"

Maybe—or maybe not.

That's the gamble college students accept when they don't take systematic notes in class. Usually, it's a risky gamble. No matter how good your memory, you start forgetting lecture material the moment a class ends. In addition, most textbooks aren't meant to contain everything you need to know about a subject area. They're meant to provide the *basis* for your courses. In class, instructors supplement the textbook material with large amounts of information gathered from their advanced study and research. They emphasize some textbook topics, give lighter treatment to others, and often introduce new ideas not covered in the text.

If you don't take class notes, or if your notes are incomplete and disorganized, you'll probably find it difficult to learn the subject matter of your courses, even if you read the textbooks with great care. Good notes, however, can help you both to learn the subject matter and to demonstrate your knowledge on examinations.

Overview and Benefits

This chapter offers a four-part approach to building better skills in taking and using class notes. First, you'll read about several popular styles or methods for taking notes. Sample notes are included to show how lecture material can be effectively recorded in different ways. Next, you'll learn how to prepare yourself for class and for taking useful notes. Skill Builder 6 will give you practice in one of the essential processes involved in note taking.

Then, you'll get some tips on listening to, understanding, and recording the information presented in class. Skill Builder 7 will help you sharpen your ability to detect and interpret the oral signals that instructors provide when lecturing and leading class discussions. Finally, you'll read a few suggestions about how to put your class notes to good use once you've recorded them.

There are a number of ways that improved note taking skills can work to your advantage both in college and in your future activities.

- You'll learn more from each class session and will acquire a better understanding of your courses than you could get from the textbooks alone.
- You'll feel more involved with the subject matter and with the challenge of learning it. As a result, the time you spend in class will become more meaningful to you. This can help you improve your attitude toward any courses that aren't very interesting to you.
- You'll have, in the form of your notes, comprehensive outlines to use when studying for exams. With effort and practice, you can improve your grades over time.
- You'll develop a valuable *life skill* that can prove useful in a variety of out-of-class activities, such as in recording the main items of discussion at meetings of the social, political, or extracurricular groups you might join on campus. You'll also find this skill useful after graduation—for instance, in taking down instructions for performing on-the-job tasks.

Checking Your Present Skills

The Self-Help Checklist that follows will get you started on thinking about your present skills, habits, and attitudes related to class notes. Read each of the ten statements carefully and then mark your answer. Circle the letter "T" if the statement is *true* for you. Circle "F" if the statement is *false* for you.

Mark the answers that accurately describe your approach to taking and using class notes—even if, in some instances, your answers differ from obviously "correct" answers. This checklist is for your use only, and no one else need see your answers. Be sure to respond to all ten statements.

Self-Help Checklist:
Taking Class Notes

1. **T** **F** When I review my class notes, I try to give extra attention to points that the instructor emphasized.

2. **T** **F** My class notes often tend to get disorganized as the academic term progresses.

3. **T** **F** When I take notes in class, I try to copy the instructor's exact words.

4. **T** **F** I usually begin each study session by reviewing and expanding the notes I took in class.

5. **T** **F** I feel that there's not much point in taking class notes if I've read the textbook assignment on the material being covered.

6. **T** **F** I usually don't review my class notes until it's time to study for an exam.

7. **T** **F** When taking notes in class, I often find it hard to know what to write down and what to leave out.

8. **T** **F** When I take class notes, I copy important equations, diagrams, or graphs that the instructor puts on the board.

9. **T** **F** My note taking system allows me to distinguish main points from minor details.

10. **T** **F** I usually compare my class notes with the textbook material covering the same topic.

- Statements 1, 4, 8, 9, and 10 are almost always *true* for students with good skills and habits in note taking and positive attitudes about the process.
- Statements 2, 3, 5, 6, and 7 are almost always *false* for students with good skills and habits in note taking and positive attitudes about the process.

What Do You Need to Work On?

The statements in the Self-Help Checklist are based on specific skills, habits, and attitudes that present problems for many college students. Look back over your answers to see how they compare with the key below the checklist.

As you do so, reread the ten statements. Ask yourself which of your skills, habits, or attitudes related to class notes need the most attention. The suggestions on the following pages can help you with all of the matters covered in the checklist—and quite a few more.

Learning a Note Taking Method

The purpose of taking notes is to record the main ideas of a lecture, class discussion, or other presentation so that, later (typically in preparing for an exam), you'll be able to review, recall, and mentally reconstruct the information that was presented. Unless you have an organized method, though, your notes won't be very helpful when you try to reconstruct information presented to you weeks or months earlier. If your notes are incomplete or poorly organized, if they don't make sense when you review them later, you could probably benefit by learning and using a proven note taking method.

There are many effective methods for taking notes. Regardless of the style or format involved, all good note taking methods have four features in common.

- They *highlight* the main ideas covered in a lecture or other presentation of information.
- They *show the relationships* among the main ideas.
- They *organize* the minor points, details, facts, and examples that support each main idea.
- They *remind you* of your assignments and due dates and of any extra readings recommended by your instructors.

Several widely used methods of taking notes are described on the following pages—outline style (both traditional and modified), diagram notes, and the Cornell System. Sample notes are provided to illustrate that there is no single best method. In fact, as the sample notes show, the same material can be recorded equally well in a number of ways. The task for you is to select a note taking method that you feel comfortable with, one that promises to work effectively for you. When you've selected a method, use it daily in your courses and make an all-out effort to master it. In Skill Builder 6, you'll have a chance to practice something that's basic to all organized note taking systems—classifying information according to its importance and degree of detail.

If you'd like to learn more about styles or methods for taking notes, or if you feel that you could use some coaching on your note taking procedures, check with the academic advising center or learning skills lab on your campus.

1. Outline Notes

Traditional outline notes (Figure 3.1) are among the most effective note taking styles—and the most difficult to learn. The advantage of outline notes is that their highly organized structure makes them ideal to use in reviewing for exams. The disadvantage is that many students have difficulty with, or are put off by, the numbering and lettering associated with traditional outline notes. Sometimes, students who try outline notes find that the effort required to get the numbering and lettering right distracts them from concentrating on the lecture.

However, with *modified outline notes* (Figure 3.2), it isn't necessary to number or letter every entry. The relationships among the entries in the notes are made clear by the careful use of indentations. Main topics or points start at the far left of the page. Subtopics are indented beneath the main topics. *Sub*subtopics and details are indented still further, and so forth.

If you are systematic about your use of indentation, you can probably do without lettering and numbering most of the time. An obvious exception would be material that naturally lends itself to being numbered. For example, if your instructor says that there are "three causes," "four phases," or "five outcomes" that you need to know about, it would make sense to number the main entries in your notes on that material.

Both traditional and modified outline styles can be beneficial because they require you to concentrate fully on the lecture or other presentation and to evaluate what you're hearing. You must listen carefully for your instructor's oral signals (discussed later in this chapter) that mark causation, subordination, transitions, and other relationships among the ideas presented. Outline style works best with instructors who are highly organized, and perhaps even a bit formal, in their presentation of lecture material. Outlining doesn't work quite as well with instructors who are disorganized or who favor spontaneous, rambling lectures. In addition, the method may not work well in some free-ranging discussion classes.

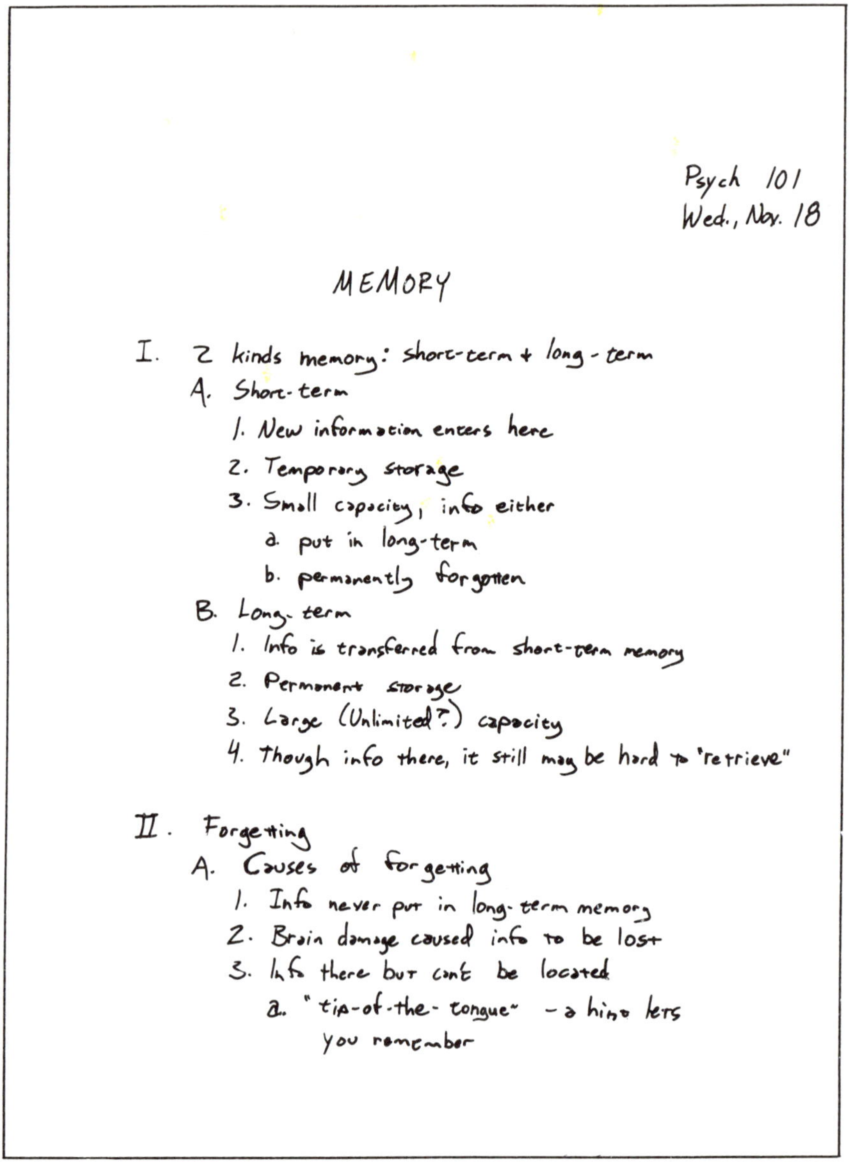

Psych 101
Wed., Nov. 18

MEMORY

I. 2 kinds memory: short-term + long-term
   A. Short-term
      1. New information enters here
      2. Temporary storage
      3. Small capacity, info either
         a. put in long-term
         b. permanently forgotten
   B. Long-term
      1. Info is transferred from short-term memory
      2. Permanent storage
      3. Large (Unlimited?) capacity
      4. Though info there, it still may be hard to "retrieve"

II. Forgetting
   A. Causes of forgetting
      1. Info never put in long-term memory
      2. Brain damage caused info to be lost
      3. Info there but can't be located
         a. "tip-of-the-tongue" – a hint lets you remember

Figure 3.1. Traditional Outline Notes

b. Other info in way (learning Spanish may make French vocab. harder to remember)

c. Painful memories sometimes seem to be "shut away"

d. Electric stimulation of brain - may vividly "relive" past experiences not otherwise available

B. Improving memory

1. Be sure to get info into long-term memory

a. Process info - do something with it

① Ask self questions on material just read

② Do practice probs using formula just learned

b. Overlearn - don't stop when you barely know something

2. To find info in long-term memory

a. Use mental cues (like HOMES to remember names of Gt. Lakes)

b. Practice recalling info at intervals

Assignment - Read Chapt. 4 for Friday

Figure 3.1 (cont'd.). Traditional Outline Notes

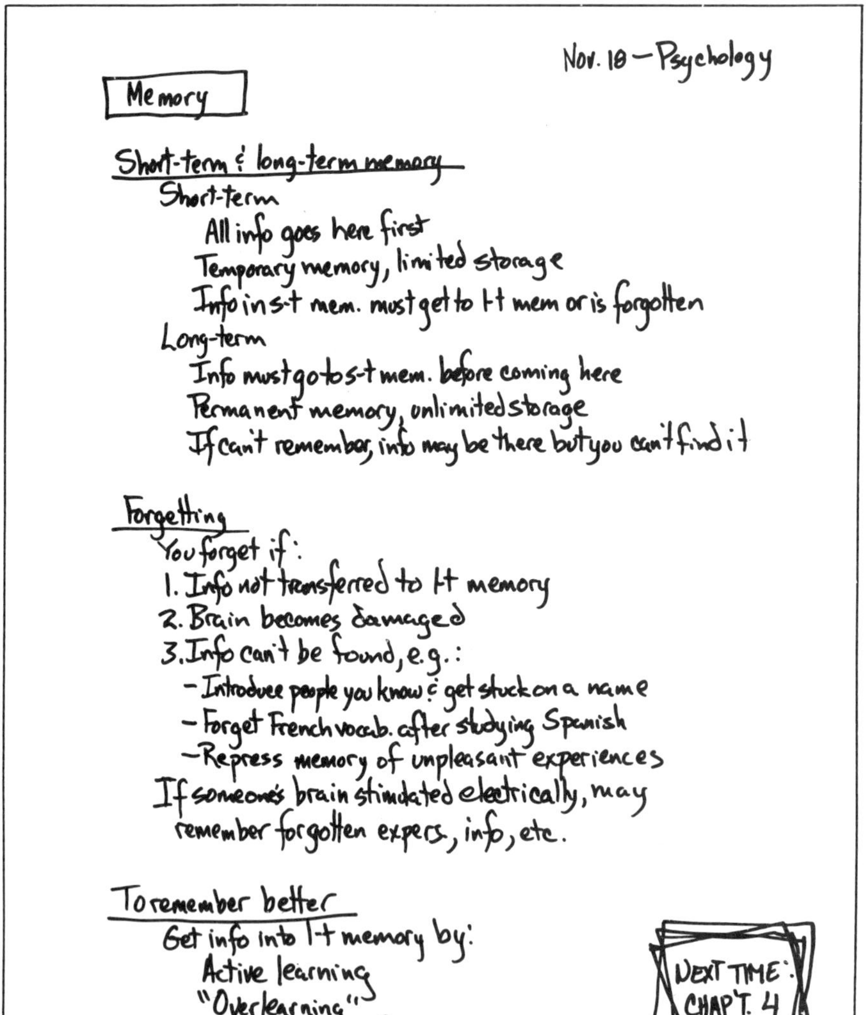

Nov. 10 — Psychology

Memory

Short-term & long-term memory
Short-term
All info goes here first
Temporary memory, limited storage
Info in s-t mem. must get to l-t mem or is forgotten
Long-term
Info must go to s-t mem. before coming here
Permanent memory, unlimited storage
If can't remember, info may be there but you can't find it

Forgetting
You forget if:
1. Info not transferred to l-t memory
2. Brain becomes damaged
3. Info can't be found, e.g.:
– Introduce people you know & get stuck on a name
– Forget French vocab. after studying Spanish
– Repress memory of unpleasant experiences
If someone's brain stimulated electrically, may remember forgotten expers., info, etc.

To remember better
Get info into l-t memory by:
Active learning
"Overlearning"
Make info easier to find in l-t mem. by:
Mnemonics
Practice

NEXT TIME: CHAP'T. 4

Figure 3.2. Modified Outline Notes

2. Diagram Notes

Diagram notes—sometimes called schematic or pictorial notes—are another good way to record the information presented in lectures and other classes. Chances are, you already take diagram notes, on a limited basis, in certain kinds of courses. For instance, it's not unusual for students in biology, economics, geology, and physics to copy diagrams, graphs, or other illustrations into their notes.

Diagram notes can also be used to record the more "textual" kind of information presented in courses like English, history, philosophy, and sociology. There are several methods for "mapping" and making tree-like diagrams of this kind of lecture material. However, the benefits of such methods may be outweighed by the considerable time and effort required to learn them.

A simple method of diagram note taking is called the *T-outline* or *T-notes* (Figure 3.3). As the name suggests, T-notes involve recording information around one or more large T's that you draw on the page of your class notebook. Each main idea or topic goes above the top of a T. The subtopics or key points are recorded on the left one-half of the page as the instructor introduces them. For each subtopic or key point, the details, examples, and other supporting information are recorded on the right of the page.

The T-note style is easy to learn and use. It can allow you a good deal of flexibility in adjusting to different courses. In some courses, for instance, you may need only a single T for an entire lecture. In other courses, you may need several T's for a lecture, each T covering a separate idea or topic. If you try T-notes, you'll quickly learn to adapt the method to the amount and complexity of the information presented and to the degree of detail.

One helpful feature of T-notes is that the format sets aside space at the top of the T for a brief summary of the main idea. This is handy because it's often hard to tell what the main idea of a lecture or discussion is until you've listened carefully for several minutes. When the main idea isn't quite clear, or you haven't yet decided how to sum it up in a few words, you can leave the top of the T blank until later in the class. Meanwhile, continue taking notes on the subtopics and supporting details. When the main idea becomes clear to you, go back and fill in the top of the T.

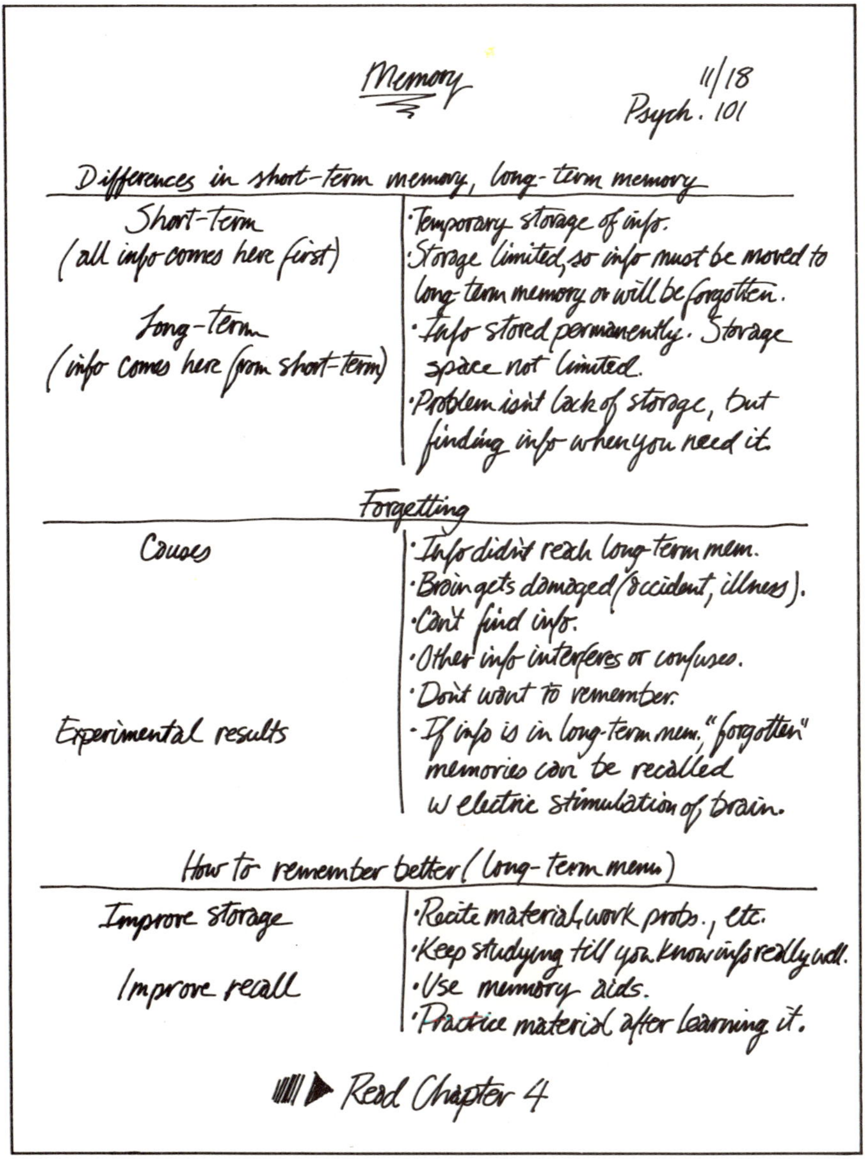

Memory

11/18
Psych. 101

Differences in short-term memory, long-term memory

Short-Term (all info comes here first)	·Temporary storage of info. ·Storage limited, so info must be moved to long-term memory or will be forgotten.
Long-term (info comes here from short-term)	·Info stored permanently. Storage space not limited. ·Problem isn't lack of storage, but finding info when you need it.

Forgetting

Causes	·Info didn't reach long-term mem. ·Brain gets damaged (accident, illness). ·Can't find info. ·Other info interferes or confuses. ·Don't want to remember.
Experimental results	·If info is in long-term mem. "forgotten" memories can be recalled w electric stimulation of brain.

How to remember better (long-term mem.)

Improve storage	·Recite material, work probs., etc. ·Keep studying till you know info really well.
Improve recall	·Use memory aids. ·Practice material after learning it.

Read Chapter 4

Figure 3.3. Diagram Notes (T-Note Style)

3. Cornell System Notes

The *Cornell System* (Figure 3.4) is more than just a note taking style or method. It's a complete set of procedures for recording and *using* class notes effectively. If, after reading the description that follows, you want to learn more about the Cornell System, see your academic advising center or learning skills lab. Or check out a book that treats the subject in detail.

The Cornell System calls for a special page format. You create the format by drawing a vertical line down each right-hand page in your class notebook. This line should be 2½″ in from the left edge of the page and should stop 2″ (or more) from the bottom of the page. Then draw a horizontal line to mark off the bottom 2″ or so of the page. Record your notes in the 6″-wide area to the right of the vertical line. Take outline notes, paragraph notes, sentence notes, or whatever else works best for you.

After class, use the *recall column* to the left of the vertical line for writing down the key words and phrases from your notes. Then, on each page of notes for that day's lecture, cover the material to the right of the vertical line. Using the key words and phrases in the recall column as memory cues, test yourself by reciting the main ideas and supporting details of the lecture in your own words. Check your responses against your notes. Brush up on any areas or topics where your responses weren't complete and accurate.

Next, read through all of the key words and phrases in the recall columns for that set of notes to perfect your understanding of how the main ideas or topics of the lecture fit together and form a logical whole. Finally, write a brief summary of the material in the *summary area* that you marked off at the bottom of each page. The act of thinking out and writing these Cornell summaries greatly reinforces your learning of the main ideas. Also, when you prepare for examinations, you'll find that the summaries often suggest answers to likely exam questions.

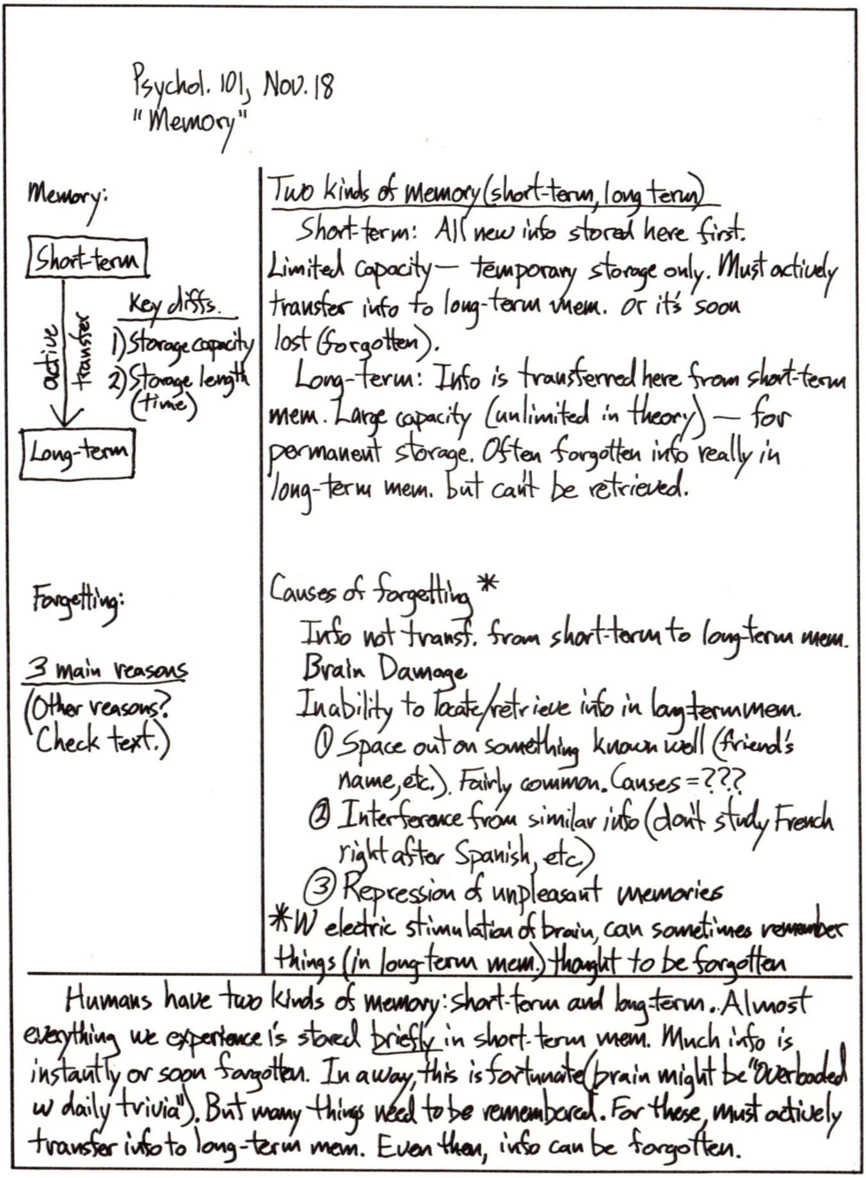

Figure 3.4. Cornell System Notes (with recall column and summary area filled in after class)

Psychol. 101, Nov. 18
"Memory" – pg. 2

Recall column	Notes
Improving memory:	<u>Ways to improve memory</u>
	Measures to ensure transf. of info to long-term mem.
<u>2 main ways</u>	① Active processing of info: Recite/review info just learned. Quiz self. Do exercises, problems, etc. ("Act on the info.")
1) Better transfer/storage in long-term (2 examples)	② Overlearning of material (beyond basic knowl.)
2) Better locating/retrieving in long-term (2 examples)	Measures to help locate/retrieve info in long-term mem.
	① Mnemonic devices ("HOMES," etc.)
	② Frequent practice in recalling/using the info
	Study Ch. 4 for 11/20 Class

People can <u>train</u> themselves to remember better (more info, longer memory, faster/more accurate recall, etc.). Main ways are through improving transfer/storage of info (in long-term mem.), also improving location/retrieval of info.

Figure 3.4 (cont'd.). Cornell System Notes (with recall column and summary area filled in after class)

Summary:
Learning a Note Taking Method

1. **Traditional outline notes** can be highly effective, although many students have trouble with the numbering and lettering required. **Modified outline notes** can be a good alternative. They do away with most of the numbering and lettering, and highlight the organization of topics and subtopics through careful use of indentation.

2. **Diagram notes** can be helpful to some students in certain kinds of courses but probably are too specialized for general use. **T-notes,** a simplified form of diagram notes, are relatively easy to learn and use.

3. **Cornell System notes** involve both a special page format and a set of review, self-test, and summary procedures aimed at total mastery of classroom material. For students who want a unified system for recording and using notes, this method offers many advantages.

Preparing for Class

Like any other process that requires concentration and mental effort, taking good notes in class will come more easily if you're well prepared. When you go to class fully prepared to learn, you get more out of your lectures, labs, and discussions. In addition, your class notes will be more meaningful and far more useful to you later when you review for exams. This section of the chapter presents four suggestions that can help you in preparing yourself for class.

1. Keep up With Assignments

College courses are often planned in such a way that each class session builds on the previous reading assignment or other outside work. It makes good sense, then, to keep up with your assignments. By doing so, you get a good introduction to the material before it's explained, elaborated on, or discussed in class. You'll be ready to understand your instructors' lectures better and to contribute more to class discussions. Because the information presented in class will not be entirely new to you, you'll find it much easier to take notes. Your notes will be better organized, more complete, and more helpful when you study for an exam.

2. Review Your Previous Notes

To master college courses, you need to see each of them as a body of logically connected ideas, not as just a grab bag of unrelated facts. One good way to discover the structure of the subject matter is to regularly review your class notes. In this way, you'll see how each class session connects with, and adds to, the material presented in earlier sessions.

When you do your reading assignment or other outside work for a course, make it a habit to start by reviewing your most recent class notes for that course. Quiz yourself on the main points covered. This practice needn't take more than five to ten extra minutes of your time. In return, it will firm up your base of knowledge for your study session—and for the next class meeting. As a result, you'll learn more in class, and your notes will more clearly show the pattern of ideas in the course.

If your instructor has handed out a syllabus or course outline, review it at least once a week. Notice how the material presented in that week's classes fits into the overall flow of the course. If you don't have a course outline, you can still get the big picture by frequently reviewing your textbook's table of contents as you read your assignments.

Just before a class, while other students are settling into their seats, quickly skim your notes from the previous meeting of that class. This will set the context for the current class session and help you to maintain continuity in your understanding of the material and in your notes.

3. Think of Questions for Class

As you review your previous notes and do your next reading assignment for a course, keep track of any questions that occur to you. If no questions arise on their own, make an effort to think of two or three that you would like to have answered during the next class meeting.

For example, if you're studying for a lecture course and you come upon something in your textbook or notes that you don't understand—or something that you simply want to know more about—be sure to write it down. In the next meeting of the class, listen extra carefully for the answer or explanation. The lecture may well deal with your question or problem in detail. If it doesn't, ask your question during class, or try to get a moment of your instructor's time right after class. If that's not possible, see your instructor during his or her office hours. Thinking of questions for lecture classes will make your studies more interesting. The process will also help you to listen more actively for answers in class.

The same principle applies to discussion classes. When something in your notes or in one of your assignments puzzles you or has special appeal for you, write a reminder to talk about it in your next class. Most instructors welcome student questions and comments as a way of getting the class interested in the material. By sharing your thoughts in class, you can help broaden discussions beyond the basic information in the textbook. This will make it easier for you to get actively involved in the course and to develop motivation for mastering the subject matter.

4. Keep Yourself Organized

Solid academic preparation will do you little good if you skip classes, show up late, or forget to bring the text, your notebook, and a pen. These may seem like small matters, but they're important ones. Unfortunately, many college freshmen have problems with them. Don't let personal disorganization prevent you from succeeding in college. Besides making it hard for you to take notes and keep up with your classmates in knowledge of the subject matter, disorganization may give your instructors the impression that you don't care about their courses. Since an instructor's *impression* of you and your degree of seriousness about the course could be the deciding factor if your grade for the term falls on the borderline, why give your instructors any reason to feel less than 100% positive about you?

In using this book, you may have noticed that every chapter so far has tried to single out some of the main differences between high school and college. These differences are important because they require great adjustments of newly admitted freshmen. Another of the main differences is the fact that, in college, no one "forces" students to attend class. As a result, some freshmen have trouble resisting the temptation to sleep through early morning classes or to skip afternoon classes when the weather is nice. Think twice before missing *any* class. In college, remember, your studies are your full-time job. Unless you are ill or have something extremely urgent to take care of, you should attend to your job every day. Anything less could put you at a disadvantage relative to other students.

If you *must* miss a class, either notify your instructor in advance or explain to the instructor before the start of the following class. Copy notes for the class you missed from a reliable classmate.

Summary:
Preparing for Class

1. Keep up with your reading and other assignments so as to preview the material that will be presented in class. This will increase your ability to understand classroom material and will simplify the process of taking organized, useful notes.

2. Review your notes regularly to see how each class session builds on the one before and to ensure that your notes connect logically with what you've learned earlier.

3. As you study, build interest and involvement in the subject matter by thinking of questions and comments to follow up on in your next classes.

4. To be fully prepared for learning and to make the right impression on your instructors, attend every class session. Don't overlook the small organizational details like taking the necessary supplies and materials.

Skill Builder 6:
Sorting Ideas by Importance

This Skill Builder will give you practice in sorting ideas according to their importance, their degree of detail, and the relationships among them—an ability that's essential in outlining and all other effective note taking methods.

INSTRUCTIONS

- Read the alphabetical list of "Types of Sports" at the top of the Outlining Worksheet on the next page. As you do so, think about how the items in the list relate to each other. Try to mentally sort out the broadest and most general items from the more specific ones.
- Fill in the numbered and lettered outline below the alphabetical list. Begin by filling in the blanks numbered I, II, and III. These are the three main divisions of the outline. The items that you choose for them should be the three broadest sport categories in the list. Be sure that your choices are broad enough to include the other items in the list. You may find it helpful to check off or line through each item as you use it in the outline.
- Then fill in the blanks lettered A and B with the six next-broadest items in the list. These are the subcategories of the three main divisions numbered I, II, and III. Make sure that each of your choices relates logically to the main division that you put it under and is broad enough to include two or three specific sports as examples.
- Finally, fill in the blanks numbered 1, 2, and 3 with the 16 most specific items in the list. These are the examples of the six subcategories lettered A and B. Make sure that each of your choices relates logically to the subcategory that you put it under.
- When you've finished, review your work to see whether it is a complete and logical outline of the items included in the list. Make certain that you haven't omitted any of the items or used any of them twice. Check your work against the answer key provided in Appendix B.

Outlining Worksheet

Types of Sports

Baseball
~~Bicycling~~
~~Contact Sports~~
~~Court Sports~~
~~Diving~~
Football
~~Handball/Racquetball~~
~~Hiking~~
~~Hockey~~
~~Individual Sports~~
~~Jogging~~
~~Land Sports~~
~~Noncontact Sports~~
~~Ping-Pong~~
~~Pool/Billiards~~
~~Soccer/Rugby~~
~~Surfing~~
~~Swimming~~
~~Table Sports~~
~~Team Sports~~
~~Tennis~~
Track and Field
~~Two- and Four-Person Sports~~
Volleyball
~~Water Sports~~

I. Individual Sports
  A. Land Sports
    1. jogging
    2. bicycling
    3. hiking
  B. Water Sports
    1. dwing
    2. surfing
    3. swimming
II. Two & Four Person Sports
  A. Court Sports
    1. handball / Raquetball
    2. Tennis
  B. Table Sports
    1. Ping-Pong
    2. Pool / Billiards
III. Team Sports
  A. Contact Sports
    1. Football
    2. Hockey
    3. Soccer / Rugby
  B. Noncontact Sports
    1. Baseball
    2. Track & Field
    3. Volleyball

Taking Notes

When done correctly, taking notes in class is not busywork and does not interfere with your ability to concentrate on the material being presented. In fact, when you know how to take notes effectively, the process actually improves your concentration and helps you to understand and remember the material better. In addition, by taking class notes you create a day-to-day course outline for use later in reviewing for exams.

In high school, many students get by with poor notes and, in some classes, with no notes at all. That practice doesn't work in college. Because of the amount of material covered in a typical college term, students *must* take notes—and good ones—in all of their courses. This can be another big adjustment for college freshmen, especially those who have limited high school experience at taking notes in fast-paced, hour-long *lecture* classes. In this section of the chapter, you'll learn ten tips for making that adjustment successfully. As you'll find out, taking meaningful and useful notes in college involves more than just good recording skills. It also requires good listening and thinking skills.

1. Use Your Note Taking Method

As you saw earlier in the chapter, it's important to learn an effective note taking method. When you have a good method, it's much easier to record the information presented in class and to organize the material into a meaningful pattern of main ideas and supporting details. No note taking method can help you, though, unless you learn it well and use it regularly.

Practice your preferred method by using it in all of your classes—not just in your lecture classes, but also in any discussion classes or lab sections that you have. You may notice that progress comes less easily in some situations than in others. That's to be expected. For instance, it can be hard at first to take organized notes on class discussions. Also, if a certain course is difficult for you, then note taking in the course will probably be difficult, too.

If you're having trouble with one of your courses, don't get discouraged. Above all, don't give up on taking notes. The more difficult a course is for you, the more you *need* good notes. Notes are vital to understanding and actively taking possession of the information presented in class. The increased comprehension and recall that you gain by taking notes, and later reviewing them, could make the difference between a superior grade and an average grade, or between passing and failing.

To sharpen your listening and recording skills, try to take notes in a variety of situations. For example, if an instructor shows a film in class, or if a student makes an oral report, take notes on the content. Because films, oral reports, and even formal speeches tend to be less structured than lectures, you'll probably find it quite a challenge to take notes on them. Making the effort, though, can improve your ability to deal with "free-form" presentations of information such as very lively class discussions and lectures given by less well organized instructors.

2. Be Neat and Orderly

Your class notes will be useful to you for later review only if you can find them and read them. Make it a point to keep your notes organized and neat. Write the date at the beginning of each set of notes you take. If you use a separate spiral-bound notebook for each of your courses, it will be easy to keep your notes for each course together and in date order. Make sure that each notebook is clearly identified on the outside by the name of the course and the section number. You may want to try a simple color-coding scheme. Keep related documents such as course outlines and other handouts in your notebooks, if that proves helpful to you.

Write or "speed-print" your notes as neatly as you can, using only the right-hand pages of your notebooks. Leaving the left-hand pages blank will make it easier for you to review and edit your notes later. The left-hand pages can be used for summary outlines, reading notes or cross-references to textbook and library material, and practice exam questions.

Take notes with a pen or a fine-tipped marker. Notes recorded with a pencil become smudged and hard to read in time. Leave wide margins at the top, bottom, and sides of each page so you'll have room to fill in and expand your notes after class. For the same reason, it's a good idea to leave extra space between the major topics or sections in your notes.

There's no firm rule about *how many* notes to record. Some students find that one page of notes per hour of class is about right. Other students need two to three pages of notes, or more, for an hour of class. As you read and begin to apply the remaining tips in this section of the chapter, you'll figure out what's best for you. In all likelihood, your answer to the question "How much is enough?" will vary from one course to another. Both the length and the degree of detail of your notes should be governed by such factors as the difficulty of the course, your background and ability in the subject area, and the grade that you want to earn.

3. Bear Down in Class

When you go to class, make an all-out effort to focus your attention on the information being presented rather than on the students around you or across the room. There's plenty of time between classes, and afterwards, to get to know the people who interest you. You'll find it easier to concentrate on the lecture or discussion if you approach each class session with a firm commitment to understanding, writing down, and remembering the main points covered.

Pick a seat where you can hear everything that's said and see both the instructor and the chalkboard. Put distracting thoughts out of mind as soon as you've greeted your friends and sat down. In the previous section, you learned that quickly skimming your notes just before the start of a class can provide you with the context for the lecture. Added benefits of this procedure are that it helps you to begin concentrating and that it allows you to avoid getting too involved in the conversations around you.

It's much easier to concentrate on academic subject matter when you're interested in the material and the process of learning it. To help yourself get into the proper mind-set, listen actively for answers to the questions that you thought of earlier while you were reviewing your notes. Remember, though, that the "answers" are less likely to be simple and direct than complex and doled out in bits and pieces. Listen extra carefully for information that isn't in the textbook or that differs from the textbook's treatment of a topic.

Another good way to remain alert in class is by listening both to learn the material presented *and* to identify possible exam questions. In discussion classes, make it a point to participate, even if you're uneasy about speaking up in a group. Think of two or three relevant questions or comments in each discussion session—and volunteer at least one of them.

Keep up your concentration until the end of class. Sometimes, when the lecturer or the discussion group has gone off on an interesting tangent early in the class session, the final ten minutes of a class may cover as much material as the preceding 40 or 50 minutes. If you've tuned out ahead of time, you're likely to miss half of the information presented in that class. When you start getting restless (or drowsy) late in a class session, change position in your chair or flex and relax your back muscles. Try to regain alertness without disturbing other students or making the instructor think that you're bored.

4. Listen Critically but With an Open Mind

Not everything you hear in a class discussion, or even in a well prepared lecture, is worth writing down and remembering. However, to catch the ideas that are worth keeping, you have to listen *critically* to everything that's said. As you listen to your instructors and classmates, you should be constantly evaluating the meaning, importance, and accuracy of their statements. You should be asking yourself whether their comments add to your understanding of the subject matter—and, if so, in what ways. You should also be asking yourself whether you agree.

If you disagree with someone's opinion, or if a particular concept or philosophy is offensive to you, keep an open mind about it. Follow the other person's line of reasoning and see where it leads you. You might discover something of value that you hadn't considered before. If not, you're always free to question the other person's point of view or to state your own. Before you can take exception with someone, though, you must first fully understand what he or she has been saying.

Finally, if for some reason you don't get along with one of your instructors, or if a certain instructor's voice or personal style annoys you, don't let that interfere with your ability to learn the material. Keep an open mind by concentrating on the message, not on your feelings about the messenger. In college, you can't afford to let anything or anyone get between you and mastery of your courses.

5. Learn Your Instructors' Signals

College instructors use a variety of signals to help students trace the logical connections among ideas and pick out the main points. This is especially true of instructors in lecture courses. For example, phrases such as "the following three factors" or "the four major causes" are intended to alert you to the importance and general organization of a body of related information that is going to be presented to you. Words like "consequently" or "therefore" signal that an effect or a result is about to be stated.

If you have trouble recognizing or interpreting signals of these kinds, you may find it helpful to review the material on "Signal Words and Phrases" in Chapter 2, Reading Textbooks (see topic 6 in the section about "How Textbooks Are Organized"). Skill Builder 7 in the present chapter also can help you develop your ability to recognize oral signals.

Repetition is another common technique for emphasizing the main points in a lecture. Repetition is so important, in fact, that some educators speak of the "law of repetition" as one of the keys to successful instruction. Train yourself to be sensitive to repetition. When you notice that a topic or point is being repeated, rephrased, or discussed in greater detail than others, assume that it's an important one.

Lecturers might also drive home their main points by decreasing the speed or increasing the volume at which they talk. Of course, not all signals are oral. Instructors often indicate that something is important by writing it on the chalkboard, tapping or underlining on the board, using a visual aid, or stepping toward the group.

Learn the general style and the specific signals of each of your instructors. When they go out of their way to make sure that everyone gets the point, there's a good reason for their doing so. Often, the reason is to help students identify material that they're likely to be tested on. Obviously, then, it's to your advantage to be alert to your instructors' signals.

As you take class notes, you might want to underline or highlight—along with other important material—topics that an instructor has emphasized. This will remind you to give the material extra attention when you study for an exam. However, don't get carried away with such markings. Until you've heard the entire lecture or discussion, you may not know for certain what's important and what isn't. For this reason, you should keep your in-class markings to a minimum. Later, when you're reviewing your notes after class, you'll be able to make more effective use of underlining or highlighting.

6. Understand Before You Write

As you've learned already, not everything said in class is worth writing down. It's neither necessary nor desirable to try to record everything you hear. If you suspect that you take too many notes or notes on the wrong things, slow down and allow yourself a chance to think about what you're hearing and to make sure that you understand it fully. You won't fall behind by occasionally putting your pen down. In fact, the greater danger lies in the opposite direction. If you take notes constantly, you may record all of the important points, but you'll probably be too busy writing to fully understand them.

Learn to rely more on the speed and power of your mind. The human brain can process incoming spoken information at about 400 words per minute. However, instructors seldom speak faster than 100 words per minute during a lecture. That's a four-to-one ratio in your favor.

So before you write, listen carefully to what's being said. Evaluate its meaning and importance. After all, how can you write a useful note about something if you haven't allowed yourself time to understand it? When you're sure that you understand, record the idea in your own words. Try to capture the main point in as few words as possible. Your notes will be shorter, less cluttered, more focused, and far more helpful when you use them to prepare for tests and exams.

7. Take Shortcuts When Possible

Being selective about what to write down is an important note taking shortcut. There are other good shortcuts that involve *how* to note material. Knowing and using these shortcuts can help all college students, particularly freshmen who are new to the note taking demands of lecture courses. Shortcuts are essential if you have a lecturer who talks very fast and rarely pauses to let students catch up.

The most obvious note taking shortcut is to avoid copying word for word or writing complete sentences. Note taking is probably the only academic activity in which your instructors will encourage you to write sentence fragments. As long as the notes make sense to you later, don't be concerned if they're not perfectly grammatical. Drop out articles like "a," "an," and "the." Skip prepositions and verbs when they can be easily inferred from the context, as in "Bill [of] Rights [is] keystone [of] personal freedoms." Delete all adjectives ("basic") and adverbs ("very") that aren't necessary for understanding the material.

Use abbreviations and symbols in your notes, but only to the extent that they speed up note taking. Don't use so many that you waste time puzzling over them when you later review your notes. Some widely known, standard abbreviations can be useful in almost any course or subject area.

&	*and*	i.e.	*that is*
e.g.	*for example*	w/	*with*
etc.	*and so forth*	w/o	*without*

You can create other abbreviations by deleting the vowels and some of the consonants from long words ("trnsptn" for "transportation"). Often, though, it's easier to shorten long words by leaving off the final syllables ("devel" for "developmental"). Use numerals instead of spelling out numeric expressions. It's quicker, for instance, to jot "3" or "3rd" than to write out "three" or "third."

Some of the operational signs that you learned in high school math can help you out in a variety of college courses. Examples of useful math-based symbols include the following.

~	*approximate(ly), about*	>	*greater than, after*
=	*equals, is (the same as)*	<	*less than, before*
≠	*doesn't equal, isn't (the same as)*	∴	*therefore, thus*

Along with such generally useful abbreviations and symbols, you'll also need some that are specific to each of your courses. You'll quickly pick up many course-specific abbreviations from your textbooks and instructors. Every economics student, for instance, knows that "gross national product" can be abbreviated "GNP." Feel free to invent other course-specific abbreviations as you need them. If your English class is going to spend a week on the works of Nathaniel Hawthorne and Herman Melville, there's no reason that you shouldn't abbreviate these authors' names (after writing out each name in full on first reference) as "NH" and "HM."

By using shortcuts like these and devising others of your own, you'll spend less time on the mechanics of note taking and have more time for listening, thinking, and understanding. The only requirements are for your notes to accurately record the main ideas presented in class—***and*** for you to be able to make sense of your notes later. If you use any abbreviations or symbols whose meanings you might later forget, be sure to write down the "code" or key to them somewhere in your notes.

8. Note Specifics

Get into the habit of writing down the highly specific information that your instructors present in class. There are three kinds of specifics that you'll need to record—oral examples, visual aids, and factual information.

Oral examples clarify abstract ideas and show how theories and principles can be applied. When your instructor offers an example, he or she is trying to help students understand a difficult concept. Take advantage of the offer and, in your notes, briefly summarize the example.

Visual aids and *factual information* are exceptions to the general rule of taking notes in your own words. In these cases, it's often important to copy the material exactly as presented by your instructor. Visual aids, whether written on the chalkboard, displayed on a poster or pull-down chart, or shown with an overhead projector, function much like oral examples. They clarify abstract ideas and help to make them concrete. Factual information—like names, dates, places, formulas, equations, and quotations—adds to and supports the major concepts that you're expected to learn. When you can't see the material, or didn't hear all of it, be sure to speak up before the instructor moves on to another topic. If that isn't possible, copy what you missed from another student during or after class.

9. Note Your Own Ideas

Don't hesitate to include your own ideas, interpretations, and questions in your notes. In a lecture, if your instructor is giving an example and you think of one that is more helpful to you personally, note *both* examples. In a class discussion, if you see a connection between ideas that your instructor and classmates haven't commented on, write it down. You might also want to share your thinking with the class. If you have a question that you plan to follow up on during your next study session or trip to the library, note that, too.

Writing down your own ideas is a good way to maintain your interest and concentration in class and to keep actively involved with the subject matter. It also helps you make sure that you're mentally processing the information you hear. Remember, though, to set off your ideas from those of the instructor, perhaps by putting yours in brackets or parentheses. In this way, you'll avoid confusion later as to *whose* ideas you've recorded.

10. Note Assignments and Suggested Readings

Write down all assignments that your instructors announce in class—whether required textbook readings, exams, papers, or special projects. Also record due dates and any other key information about the assignments. When an instructor suggests some books or journal articles for supplemental reading, copy the titles accurately. If you have time later, make an effort to at least familiarize yourself with the recommended material.

Circle all assignments and suggested readings, or highlight them in some other way, so you can pick them out easily when you start your next study session.

Summary:
Taking Notes

1. Use a proven note taking method and don't be discouraged if it works less smoothly in some courses than in others. Keep practicing. The harder a course is, the more you'll need good notes when the time comes to review for an exam.

2. Take your notes neatly, in ink, and organize them by course and date. Ideally, keep your notes for each course in a separate spiral-bound notebook. Leave extra space in each set of notes so you can edit and expand the material when you review later.

3. Keep alert in class by focusing your attention on the material to be learned. Maintain interest and concentration by listening for answers to the questions that you thought of when preparing for the class.

4. Critically evaluate the meaning and importance of what you hear, and keep an open mind about ideas that differ from yours. Don't let negative feelings about a concept, course, or instructor interfere with your concentration or cause you to stop listening.

5. Learn to recognize the signals that instructors offer to help students follow lectures, pick out main ideas, and identify likely exam questions. Carefully underline or highlight emphasized material so you can give it extra attention when you study for an exam.

6. To keep your notes short and to be certain that you really understand the information you're recording, make it a point to listen and think before you write. Then note only the key ideas, expressed in your own words.

7. Except for certain kinds of specific information, avoid word-for-word copying and keep your notes as brief as possible. Use sentence fragments, abbreviations, symbols, and other shortcuts to save time.

8. Note specifics that clarify abstract ideas or show how theories and principles are applied. Take summary notes on oral examples, but try to copy most visual aids and factual information exactly as presented.

9. To help maintain concentration and personal involvement with the subject matter, include your own ideas and questions in your notes. Bracket these or mark them in some other way that will set them off from your instructor's statements.

10. Record in your notes all required and suggested assignments, with due dates and any other key information. Highlight assignments so that you'll remember them when reviewing your notes and take prompt action.

Skill Builder 7:
Recognizing Oral Signals

This Skill Builder will help you improve your ability to recognize and understand some of the oral signals that instructors use in lectures and class discussions.

INSTRUCTIONS

- Look over the alphabetical list of "Signal Words and Phrases" at the top of the Oral Signals Worksheet on the next page. In doing so, think about what the words and phrases might tell you if an instructor used them in class.
- Assign each of the signal words and phrases to one of the six descriptive categories below the alphabetical list. Begin with the first signal ("a case in point"). Scan the six categories and write the phrase under the category that best matches its meaning.
- Do the same with the second signal ("additionally"), then the third signal, and so forth. You may find it helpful to check off or line through each signal word or phrase as you assign it to a category.
- When you're finished, review your work. You should have *three* signal words or phrases listed under each category. Pay close attention to fine differences of meaning. Some of the signal words and phrases could be assigned to more than one category. Make sure that you've assigned each signal to the category that *most closely* matches its meaning. Check your work against the answer key in Appendix B.

Oral Signals Worksheet

Signal Words and Phrases

~~a case in point~~	furthermore	~~on the other hand~~
~~additionally~~	~~however~~	~~similarly~~
~~by the same token~~	~~in conclusion~~	~~therefore~~
~~consequently~~	~~in the final analysis~~	~~thus~~
~~conversely~~	~~likewise~~	to illustrate
~~for instance~~	moreover	~~to summarize~~

Signals indicating a continuation and expansion

additionally
furthermore
moreover

Signals indicating an example

for instance
to illustrate
a case in point

Signals indicating a parallel

similarly ✓
likewise
by the same token

Signals indicating a difference or exception

conversely ✓
on the other hand
however

Signals indicating a specific result or effect

thus
therefore
consequently

Signals indicating a general wrap-up or review

in conclusion
in the final analysis
to summarize

Using Your Notes

As vital as note taking is to understanding and remembering classroom material, the recording process itself doesn't account for all of the benefits you can gain from your notes. It's important to realize that *taking* notes isn't the ultimate goal. The goal is to *have* notes and *use* them in studying for tests and exams.

This section of the chapter presents four suggestions for using your notes to make exam preparation a comfortable, daily habit rather than a panicky, last-minute ordeal. By following these suggestions, you can avoid late-night cramming and the feelings of "test anxiety" that often affect college students at midterms and finals.

1. Review Your Notes After Class

Research on the learning process has shown that most forgetting takes place right after a student's first exposure to new material. No matter how attentive you are, no matter how good your notes may be, within 24 hours you will forget much of what you learn in class unless you take active measures to transfer the material from short-term memory to long-term memory. The best such measure is to make review of your notes a *regular* part of your study schedule.

Prompt, frequent review reinforces your initial learning of new material and, to some extent, offsets the natural process of forgetting. If you make it your regular practice to review new notes while they're fresh, the information is more likely to *remain* fresh in your mind. As a result, you will understand the material better, remember more of it longer, and recall it more effectively on exams.

Get into the habit of actively reviewing your notes and quizzing yourself on their content as soon as possible after class—ideally on the same day, but definitely no later than 24 hours after taking them. The best procedure is to review notes ***immediately*** after class. Obviously, that isn't always going to be workable. But on days when you have an hour between classes, put the time to good use by reviewing your notes from the class that just ended. When that's not possible, try to review new notes during the afternoon or evening of the day on which you recorded them. If you often have trouble finding time for review, you might want to take a look back at Chapter 1, Managing Time and Environment.

Another good technique, suggested earlier in the present chapter, is to begin each study session with a review of your most recent notes in the courses that you're going to study for. Doing this provides you with the benefits of review along with a helpful warm-up activity—a way of easing yourself into the new material you're going to study.

2. Edit Your Notes as You Review

As you review your notes, edit them while your memory of the class session is still fresh and accurate. Whatever note taking style or method you use, fill in any areas where your notes seem sketchy and incomplete, or where you've used too many abbreviations. Correct any errors that you find. Use the blank spaces that you've reserved to neatly add key points, details, or examples that may have been omitted. Try to expand and clarify your notes just enough so that weeks or months later, when you're studying for an exam, the notes will enable you to mentally reconstruct the main ideas and supporting details covered in class.

It's a good idea to refer to your textbook now and then as you edit your notes. At times, you may find it helpful to add notes from a textbook to those from a class, or to write in your class notes the page numbers of related textbook passages. By comparing and cross-referencing your class notes with your reading assignments, you can greatly increase your understanding of the material covered.

In editing your notes, underline or highlight the main concepts, terms, and facts so they'll stand out when you prepare for an exam later. Use eye-catching symbols—stars, for instance—to mark material that you're likely to be tested on, especially topics that an instructor has emphasized in class. Remember, though, to exercise restraint. Too much marking defeats the intended purpose of making the essentials stand out for quick identification. If you're careful about what you underline or highlight, your markings can serve as a course outline for use in reviewing for the midterm and final exam.

Don't waste time on recopying your notes. Recopying isn't really studying. It's a mechanical act and doesn't encourage mental processing of the information. Your time and effort will be better spent on actively reviewing and editing your notes. Doing this requires you to think about the material as you go over it. Recopying is worthwhile only when an unusually hectic class session has left you with notes that are unreadable.

3. Quiz Yourself as You Review

A good way of making sure that you're really learning the material in your notes is to quiz yourself as you review. To do this, mentally convert each major topic in your notes into the kind of question that might appear on an exam. Without looking at your notes, see how well you can answer. Recite from memory, in your own words, explaining and adding details as necessary.

Then check your response against your notes. If you have answered the question accurately and completely, you're likely to do well when you're tested on the material later. If you can't provide a good answer, you'll know that you need to brush up on the topic before you move on to the next one. In this case, it might be helpful to review both your class notes on the topic *and* the related passage in your textbook.

The left-hand pages of your notebook—if you've remembered not to take notes on them in class—can be valuable in testing your knowledge as you review. Left-hand pages, as you've already seen, can be used for expanding your notes or jotting brief summaries. You can also use the space to write practice exam questions. You needn't write out the answers if you say them aloud or compose them mentally.

4. **Get Help if You Need It**

There's another advantage to regularly reviewing and editing your notes and quizzing yourself on them. If you detect a problem in your notes, or in your understanding of the material, you'll have time to take action before an exam is given. What to do about such a problem depends on how serious the problem is.

If you find an error or omission in your notes and can't remember the correct information, ask a reliable classmate or check the textbook. If you've kept up with your reading assignments and taken good notes in class but still have trouble understanding a topic, see whether your instructor has a moment to explain before or after the next class session. Most college instructors are glad to help in this way. If your instructor doesn't have time to work with you just before or after class, make an appointment to see him or her during office hours.

When you've made your best effort but just can't understand a topic presented in class or in the textbook, it's crucial to let your instructor know at once. Inability to master a major topic or skill may put you at a disadvantage for the rest of the course. Chances are, your instructor will be able to clear things up in a matter of minutes. If other students report that they are having the same trouble, your instructor may decide to back up and go over the difficult topic or material again. If you continue to have problems, ask about special tutoring as soon as possible.

Summary:
Using Your Notes

1. To improve your understanding of classroom material and to reduce forgetting, review your class notes within 24 hours of taking them. Use review as a means of easing yourself into your next study session in a given course.

2. Edit, correct, and expand your notes as you review them. Add enough detail so that, when you study later for an exam, you'll be able to mentally reconstruct the main material covered in class. Exercise restraint in your use of underlining or highlighting.

3. As you review and edit your notes, quiz yourself to make sure that you understand and will remember the material. Before you move on, give extra attention to any topic for which you can't rephrase the main points covered in class.

4. Get help at once if your reviewing points out a gap in your notes or a weakness in your knowledge of the material. Ask a classmate or check your textbook for help with routine errors, omissions, or difficulties. Talk with your instructor if you have trouble with basic understanding of the material.

Wrap-Up

This chapter has presented information about ways of improving the quality and usefulness of your class notes. In the first part of the chapter, you learned the importance of adopting and using an effective note taking method. You also looked at some sample notes that showed how different methods can be used with the same classroom material. You then read about four ways of preparing yourself for class and for the note taking process. Skill Builder 6 gave you some experience in sorting ideas by their importance, a key ability for taking well organized notes.

You also studied ten tips for improving the listening, thinking, and recording skills that you need in order to take good notes in class. In Skill Builder 7 you practiced recognizing and interpreting some of the oral signals that instructors use to help students follow the logical sequence of material presented in lectures and class discussions.

Finally, because class notes are a *means* to an end rather than an end in themselves, you learned four strategies for regularly reviewing your notes and using them to simplify the task of studying for exams.

Progress Check

This chapter has covered a lot of material. You may already have known some of it. Probably, though, much of the material was new to you. Here's your chance to check your progress and see what you've learned.

Take a few moments now to answer the seven questions that follow. Try to answer from memory, and in your own words. If you can't remember every answer, it's all right to look back through the chapter. When you're finished, check your work against the key in Appendix B.

1. What are the four features that all effective note taking systems have in common?

- highlight main ideas covered
- remind about assignments
- show relationships among ideas
- organize minor points support each main idea

2. Name three ways of keeping alert in class and maintaining your concentration.

- focus your attention
- make commitment to understand
- choose seat so hear & see well

3. At what rate, in words per minute, do people mentally process spoken information that they hear? What's the fastest rate at which instructors usually deliver lectures?

- 400 wpm
- 100 wpm

4. Name three of the shortcuts you can use in class to make note taking simpler.

- use abbreviations
- be selective about what write down
- write notes sentence fragments

5. What are four of the signal words or phrases that college instructors use to help students trace the connections among ideas in lectures and class discussions?

- consequently therefore
- conversely furthermore
- likewise On the other hand
- to illustrate to summarize etc

6. Describe three of the things students can do to improve their notes when editing and reviewing them after class.

- fill in areas where sketchy (notes)
- clarify abbreviations etc
- Correct errors - add omitted material

7. What does the word "cross-referencing" mean to you?

- read notes as well as text
when reviewing add additional info from one to the other

Next Steps

Although this chapter is about to end, you're really just beginning to improve your note taking skills. You can continue to develop them if you're willing to work hard. With effort and practice on your part, note taking can become a valuable life skill that you can use throughout the rest of your college career, in any graduate education or training that you undertake, and in your future employment.

Concentrate on strengthening those note taking skills that are most important to you right now. Then return to this chapter for more ideas when you're ready for them. Don't try to accomplish too much too fast. Instead, give yourself a realistic goal of steady, gradual improvement.

Practice your note taking skills in each of your courses. Although your overall ability in note taking will begin to improve in a short time, you may find that progress comes slower in some areas than in others. That's only natural and probably doesn't mean that there's any particular reason for concern. If you feel that you have a serious problem with taking or using class notes—or if you'd just like more information about note taking methods—check with the academic advising office or learning skills lab on your campus.

Chapter 4

Using Information Resources

Warm-Up

College students, like most other people, develop a lot of questions during the course of a week, or a day, or even an hour.

- *Where do the candidates stand on environmental issues?*
- *Is there a good personal computer available for under $1,200?*
- *Can you really avoid a cold by loading up on Vitamin C?*
- *How do starting salaries for business majors compare with those for liberal arts majors?*

None of those questions is unimportant, but for many students the biggest question that they will ask themselves during an academic term has a decidedly more urgent tone: *"How am I going to come up with 3,000 words for my research paper? What am I even going to write about?"*

Knowing how to resolve questions great and small can make life simpler and better. In addition, knowing how to resolve questions can make college less stressful and far more rewarding. The remarkable thing about many of life's questions, both personal and academic, is that you don't need to "have all the answers." You just need to know how to find them. That's what this chapter is about.

Overview and Benefits

Like many of the other skills covered in the previous chapters, the ability to use information resources effectively is among the most valuable *life skills* that a person can acquire. In the years after college, skill in using information resources can save you time, money, and energy—and improve the quality of the decisions that you make—no matter who you are, where you live, or what you do. At this point in your life, though, your main need for expertise with information resources probably relates to the research papers that your instructors assign.

This chapter focuses on understanding the resources of your college library and using them to gather information for your papers and other research projects. The chapter first describes the main kinds of information resources housed in a college library. You'll also learn the basics of finding the material and information that you need. Skill Builder 8 provides a worksheet that can help you start exploring your campus library.

The second part of the chapter offers suggestions for using the resources available to you in researching, writing, and revising papers. Skill Builder 9 includes a worksheet for evaluating your papers.

Good skills with information resources are vital for success in college and beyond. If you're willing to make the effort to develop your skills, you can benefit from this chapter in at least three ways.

- You'll prepare better papers for your courses. With practice, you should be able to improve your grades on such written work.
- By learning how to get an early start, you'll avoid the last-minute panic that many students experience in researching and writing papers.
- You'll know how to get the facts that you need to make major life decisions (for instance, the choice of a career or the purchase of a car) and to be an informed citizen.

Checking Your Present Skills

The Self-Help Checklist that follows will get you started on thinking about your present skills, habits, and attitudes related to using information resources. Read each of the ten statements carefully and then mark your answer. Circle the letter "T" if the statement is *true* for you. Circle "F" if the statement is *false* for you.

Mark the answers that accurately describe your approach to using information resources—even if, in some cases, your answers differ from obviously "correct" ones. This checklist is for your use only. No one else need see your answers. Be sure to respond to all ten statements.

Self-Help Checklist:
Using Information Resources

1. T F I don't fully understand the information included on a library catalog card.

2. T F I separate fact from opinion when reading books or periodicals.

3. T F I find that the microfiche reading machine allows me to access information efficiently.

4. T F I have a difficult time using reference materials other than dictionaries or encyclopedias.

5. T F I can locate a book on the library shelves when I have its call number.

6. T F When researching a paper or other assignment, I try to draw information from a variety of sources.

7. T F I review and revise my papers before I hand them in.

8. T F I'm uncertain about the differences between popular and scholarly publications.

9. T F I tend to put off work on papers until it's almost too late.

10. T F I'm not very familiar with indexes to periodicals.

- Statements 2, 3, 5, 6, and 7 are almost always *true* for students with good skills and habits in use of information resources and positive attitudes about the process.
- Statements 1, 4, 8, 9, and 10 are almost always *false* for students with good skills and habits in use of information resources and positive attitudes about the process.

What Do You Need to Work On?

The statements in the Self-Help Checklist are based on specific skills, habits, and attitudes that present problems for many college students. Look back over your answers to see how they compare with the key below the checklist.

As you do so, reread the ten statements. Ask yourself which of your skills, habits, or attitudes related to information resources need improving. The following pages cover all of the matters included in the checklist—and many more.

Exploring Your College Library

Although college libraries can seem confusing if you don't know your away around, they are in fact very orderly places. The purpose of a college library is to provide faculty and students with the best of what's been published in their fields of study. In most fields of study, published information exists in certain basic formats. College libraries organize their collections along those lines:

- Scholarly books;
- Periodicals (newspapers, magazines, and scholarly journals);
- Reference materials;
- Other resources.

In this part of the chapter, each of these four main kinds of information resources will be discussed in turn. Although no library can be expected to offer everything that will be mentioned here, all libraries try to acquire the materials that their students need most often. Many two-year colleges and smaller four-year colleges have arrangements with larger institutions nearby so that students can use a full range of library materials.

Spend some time in your college library and begin exploring its resources. (If you're eligible to use a separate departmental library or reading room, you might want to explore that, too.) Almost all college libraries provide fact sheets, floor plans, and other handouts to help newcomers find their way around. Some libraries offer leaflets that students can use to conduct self-guided tours. Be sure to ask whether such materials are available at your library.

As you're exploring your library, get to know some of the reference librarians. Reference librarians are highly skilled in helping students use correct research techniques to identify and locate information. They are also sensitive to the needs of freshmen, most of whom are awed by their first exposure to college research assignments—and to the college library.

Scholarly Books

Scholarly books are among the resources that college students most often use for their papers and other research projects. In the library of a small college, the collection of books (both scholarly and popular) may total in the scores of thousands. In a large university library, the collection may total a million volumes or more.

In either setting, it can be quite a challenge for a student to determine:

- What books are available.
- Which books might help with his or her research topic.
- How and where to find the books that might help.

Handling such challenges becomes easier once you learn how to use the catalog.

The Catalog

Every library has a catalog that lists and briefly describes all of the scholarly and popular books that the library owns. In the past, library catalogs have consisted of small paper cards arranged alphabetically in file drawers. Today, many libraries are replacing their card-based paper catalogs with computer-based electronic catalogs. You may encounter either or both kinds at your college.

As the main device for finding your way into the vast store of information available in books, a library's catalog is probably its most important research tool. The catalog lists both *circulating books* (which can be checked out) and *reference books* (which must be used in the library).

Using the Catalog

There are two keys to using a catalog, whether on cards or on a computer terminal. The first is to know that all books are listed at least twice—by author and by title. Nonfiction books also are listed by their main subject or subjects (see Figures 4.1, 4.2, and 4.3).

HF 5381 B63512

Bolles, Richard Nelson.
The three boxes of life and how to get out of them: an introduction to life/work planning. Berkeley, CA: Ten Speed Press, 1978, 1981.
466p. 23cm.

1. Vocational guidance. 2. Continuing education. 3. Retirement. 4. Success. I. Title.

Figure 4.1. Author Card

The three boxes of life and how to get out of them.

HF 5381 B63512

Bolles, Richard Nelson.
The three boxes of life and how to get out of them: an introduction to life/work planning. Berkeley, CA: Ten Speed Press, 1978, 1981.
466p. 23cm.

1. Vocational guidance. 2. Continuing education. 3. Retirement. 4. Success. I. Title.

Figure 4.2. Title Card

SUCCESS.

HF 5381 B63512

Bolles, Richard Nelson.
The three boxes of life and how to get out of them: an introduction to life/work planning. Berkeley, CA: Ten Speed Press, 1978, 1981.
466p. 23cm.

1. Vocational guidance. 2. Continuing education. 3. Retirement. 4. Success. I. Title.

Figure 4.3. Subject Card

The second key is knowing that all listings are arranged in alphabetical order. This can be trickier than it sounds. For instance, some libraries might list "Automobile tires" before "Automobiles—accidents," while others might not. Ask a librarian, or look around for written instructions, for pointers on how listings are alphabetized in your library's catalog.

The fact that the catalog contains two or more listings for each book allows you several ways of finding books. If you want a specific book, you can easily look it up by its author or title. Often, though, you'll be searching the catalog by *subject.* You'd use this approach when you're browsing for a research topic, or when you've chosen one and are determining what books might help you with it.

Here are some tips for looking up books by author, title, or subject.

- When looking up a book by **author,** look under the author's last name: "Hemingway, Ernest." You might also find listings under "Hemingway, Ernest M., 1899-" and "Hemingway, Ernest, 1899-1961." Look through all of the possibilities if you have trouble finding what you want.
- When looking up a book by **title,** ignore articles ("a," "an," "the") when they are the first word of the title. *The Sun Also Rises* will be listed under S, not T.
- When looking up a book by **subject,** be specific in defining the subject. For instance, if you're searching for information on uses of lasers in health care, your best bet probably would be to look first under the *subject heading* "Laser." (On subject cards, the subject heading is shown on the top line in red letters or all capitals.) "Health Care," "Medicine," or "Medical Technology" could prove too broad. You might find hundreds of entries to sort through.

  Subject searches can be difficult when you're just starting out. Keep trying if your first few attempts don't turn up what you need. Checking for *cross-references* to related subjects can make the task easier. For instance, if you were searching for material under the subject heading "Movies," you probably wouldn't find any listings. However, you probably *would* find a helpful cross-reference similar to one of these: "Movies—see Motion Pictures" or "Movies—see Moving-pictures." You'd then know to look under either the subject heading "Motion Pictures" or (in some libraries) the subject heading "Moving-pictures."

  Subject subheadings also can be helpful. If your topic is related to the Civil War, for example, you'll get better results under the subheading "United States — History — Civil War, 1861-1865" than under the heading "United States — History."

Many libraries have a guide called the *Library of Congress Subject Headings.* This guide lists all of the subject headings used by the Library of Congress and numerous other libraries. For each subject heading listed, the guide shows all subheadings that it includes. The guide also gives cross-references to related subject headings and to broader subject headings. The *Library of Congress Subject Headings* may be hard to use at first, but it can greatly simplify the process of searching the catalog by subject.

Whether you're searching by author, title, or subject, make sure to read and evaluate the information you find in the catalog. This will give you a rough idea of how helpful a book might be in your research. Among the items of information likely to appear on the catalog card or screen display are: author, title, main subject(s), publisher, date and place of publication, and number of pages. If a book has a bibliography or an index, that will be noted, too.

Finding What You Need in the Stacks

When you decide that you want to look at a book that's described on a card or screen, record the information that you'll need to locate the book in the *stacks.* (The stacks are the shelves where books are stored.) Copy the title of the book and the name of the author. Also copy the *call number*—the lines of letters and numbers in the upper left corner of the card. In a computer catalog, the call number may appear in a different area of the screen.

Look around for charts or floor plans that show where books with various call numbers are located in the stacks. Then go after the books that you need. Although one of the purposes of the call number system is to ensure that similar kinds of books are grouped together, be prepared to look around a little. If a book has been misshelved, it may be several volumes or several feet away from the location that the call number would lead you to expect. Even when you find what you're looking for, it's a good idea to check books shelved nearby. You may find something that covers your topic better than the book that you thought you wanted.

Periodicals

Next to scholarly books, periodicals probably will be the most useful information resources for your research papers. Periodicals include newspapers, magazines, and scholarly journals. This section will deal primarily with journals, because new college freshmen rarely know much about them.

Newspapers and magazines are considered popular or general-interest periodicals. They contain articles, stories, and other features written for broad, mixed audiences. *Newsweek, PC Magazine, Psychology Today,* and *The Washington Post* are well known examples of popular periodicals. Even such "serious" periodicals as *National Geographic* and *Scientific American* are considered popular rather than scholarly.

Scholarly journals, on the other hand, contain articles written by and for specialists in various academic subject areas and in other research professions. (Some scholarly journals are referred to as "technical," "specialized," or "professional.") A journal article communicates the opinions, theories, or research findings of the author(s) to other experts in a field. The *American Historical Review, Human Learning,* and the *Journal of the American Dietetic Association* are examples of scholarly or professional journals.

The information in a recent issue of a journal is likely to be more up to date than that in a newly published book. For this reason, journals are useful in researching very current topics. Books, however, generally deal with broader subjects in greater depth. They may offer you a better understanding of your research topic than would be possible with journal articles alone. Your instructors probably will urge you—or require you—to use both scholarly books *and* scholarly journals in your research. To identify journal articles on your research topic, you must learn how to use indexes.

Indexes

Just as the library's catalog allows you to access information in books, so indexes can help you find what you need in journals and other periodicals.

In high school, many students become familiar with the *Readers' Guide to Periodical Literature,* perhaps the most widely used index to popular periodicals. The *Readers' Guide* lists thousands of articles, by subject and by author, in alphabetical order. The specialized, subject-specific indexes that you'll be using to identify journal articles in college are arranged more or less like the *Readers' Guide.* Most of them are just as easy to use.

Examples of specialized indexes are *Art Index, Chemical Abstracts, Humanities Index,* and *Social Sciences Index.* An index whose title includes the word *Abstracts* not only lists articles but also provides a brief abstract (or summary) of each.

Using Indexes

Some specialized indexes list articles only by subject. Others list articles by subject and by author. Either way, the listings provide the information you'll need to find specific articles in the library: subject, title, author's name, name of the journal in which the article appeared, volume number and date of the journal, and page numbers of the article.

When you find an index listing for an article of possible use, read the entire listing carefully. If an abstract is included, a close reading of that should make it clear whether or not the article will help with your research topic. Spending a little extra time "up front" on indexes can save you a lot of time and effort later when you begin to locate and read the articles themselves.

Copy the identifying information just as you would when using the catalog to find books. To be on the safe side, you'll probably need to copy just about everything except the abstract.

As you start to locate the articles that you need, bear in mind that libraries offer both *current periodicals* (copies printed during the current year and stored individually) and *bound periodicals* (prior-year copies that have been bound together in book form). It's not unusual for current periodicals to be shelved in a different area of the library from bound periodicals. The checkout policies may differ, too.

Reference Materials

Unlike most books and journal articles, reference materials are not meant to be read all the way through. They're meant to be *referred to* for the items of information that you need. In a good reference collection, you can find everything from baseball statistics to U.S. tax law summaries. Usually, reference materials are kept together in their own section of the library. You can use them in the library, but you won't be allowed to check them out.

In many reference books, the contents are in alphabetical order so that users can look up what they need quickly and easily. A dictionary is perhaps the best known example of this kind of reference book. Other reference books—almanacs, for instance—don't present their contents in alphabetical order. To make it easy for users to find what they need, a reference book of this kind will have a detailed index of topics.

Although you couldn't write a college research paper just with reference materials, they can be helpful at all stages of your research. If you're stuck for ideas, thumbing through certain kinds of references can encourage creative thinking about topics. Other references can help you out with matters of spelling, grammar, punctuation, and style. And when you're looking for just the right fact, statistic, or quotation to bear out a key point in your paper, there are still other references that can provide exactly what you need.

The next two pages describe a few common reference materials.

1. **Bibliographies**

A bibliography is an alphabetical list of books or articles, usually dealing with a particular subject area. Thus, bibliographies suggest sources that you can check for published information on given topics.

While short bibliographies often appear at the end of books and journal articles, the bibliographies in a library reference collection are likely to be entire books in themselves. A good example of this kind of bibliography is *Books in Print,* which lists all books (whether new or old) that are currently available from publishers in the United States. If you've worked through the card catalog and the right indexes but can't find enough information on your topic, a bibliography might help.

2. **Encyclopedias**

Encyclopedias offer articles on a wide variety of events, topics, and people. Subject encyclopedias provide more detailed information than do general encyclopedias like the *Britannica* and the *World Book.* Some commonly used subject encyclopedias are the *Encyclopedia of Psychology,* the *Guide to American Law,* and the *McGraw-Hill Encyclopedia of Science and Technology.*

Encyclopedias can be good sources of starter ideas and background information for research. In addition, the bibliographies that they include can provide leads to more scholarly articles and books. However, in college—unlike in many high schools—encyclopedias aren't acceptable sources of core information for research papers. In other words, your research may begin among the encyclopedias, but it must not end there.

3. **Dictionaries**

These are your best sources of information about spelling, meaning, and pronunciation of words. Along with English dictionaries, a college reference collection will include foreign-language and bilingual dictionaries (English-Spanish, for instance). Your library may also offer such subject-specific works as *Stedman's Medical Dictionary.*

4. Atlases and Gazetteers

These resources provide maps and information on the geography of continents, countries, states, and cities. Information is included on location and size, terrain, climate, population, culture, economics, etc. A gazetteer is a geographical dictionary.

5. Almanacs

Because these references are published annually, much of their content is quite up to date. The information is usually presented in brief, "facts at a glance" summaries. You might use an almanac to look up last year's Gross National Product. However, for an in-depth treatment of GNP, you'd need to use books or journal articles.

Loose-leaf services, such as *Congressional Quarterly Weekly Report* and *Facts on File,* provide information even more up to date than that in almanacs and other annuals.

6. Directories

Directories are available on all kinds of people, places, and things. Directories usually provide brief descriptive listings, along with an address and phone number for each.

Biographical directories, such as *Current Biography* and *Who's Who in America,* list people who are notable for one reason or another. The *Encyclopedia of Associations* lists thousands of nonprofit groups involved in a wide variety of activities. Other directories—such as *Information USA,* the *U.S. Government Manual,* and the *Washington Information Directory*—describe branches of the federal government.

Other Library Resources

Following are descriptions of some of the other materials, equipment, and services that your library may offer. Be sure to ask about what's available, where it's located, and how to use it.

1. Reserve Collection

At almost all college libraries, instructors may put *on reserve* the books and journal articles that they assign as extra reading for their students. Often, this ever-changing collection is housed together in a special reserve room. In some libraries, students may ask for what they need at the reserve desk.

Because of the high demand for reserve materials, they're usually subject to different rules than a library's main collection. If your library allows checkout of reserve materials, it's likely to be for a period of days or hours rather than weeks.

2. Computers

Many colleges are making efforts to help their students develop working knowledge of computers. Microcomputers or computer terminals might be available for student use in your school's library. If not, the staff probably will be able to direct you to "hands-on" computer resources somewhere else on campus.

If you haven't yet acquired basic computer skills, make it a point to do so early in college. Increasingly, the kinds of jobs sought by college graduates require experience or familiarity with computers. The ability to use computers is becoming another of the life skills that have been identified throughout this book. While you're in college, knowing how to work with a computer can speed up and simplify the task of writing and revising research papers.

3. Nonprint Materials

In many libraries, information in formats other than ink-on-paper is housed together. Words like "nonprint," "audiovisual," or "microtext" may be used to identify these materials in your library. A nonprint collection might include any of the following: microfiche, microfilm, slides, videotapes, films, musical and spoken-word recordings, and computer software—*plus* the equipment needed to use these materials.

Microfiche and microfilm are systems of storing printed information in very small size. A microfiche card is only 4½″ x 6″, but one or two of them can hold the contents of an entire newspaper, magazine, or journal. Locate the microfiche or microfilm reading machines in your library and learn how to use them. Often, back issues of newspapers and magazines are available only on microfiche or microfilm.

A new system known as CD-ROM (compact disc—read-only memory) has begun to appear in some libraries. This system is based on compact discs similar to those used for recordings of music. In the case of CD-ROM, however, the discs are used to store texts. Accessing these texts requires a special kind of disc player that, typically, is used with a microcomputer.

Many standard reference works—such as *Grolier's Encyclopedia* and *Bartlett's Familiar Quotations*—are available on CD-ROM. As greater numbers of references are put onto CD-ROM, the system will find its way into more reference or nonprint collections. Indexes also are being published on CD-ROM.

4. Recreational Reading

College libraries try to provide students with a wide range of high quality publications for recreational reading and general information. Your library has a collection of fiction and other popular books and probably subscribes to leading U.S. newspapers and magazines. Chances are, indexes to newspapers and magazines are located in the library, perhaps along with special indexes for finding book reviews of interest. Newspapers and magazines published in other countries might be available, too.

5. On-Line Research Services

On-line research services usually take the form of electronic indexes and other data bases running on mainframe computers in major cities. The information stored by these services can be accessed, over telephone lines, from computer terminals around the world.

In some colleges that offer access to on-line services, this resource is mainly for the use of advanced students and faculty members. Still, if you're an underclassman with a specialized research topic, *and* you've worked through all local resources, you might ask about researching on line. You'll probably be required to pay a fee for the service.

6. And Just About Everything Else Under the Sun

Although no library will have every kind of information resource, *your* library may offer one or more of the following.

- Information on campus and community services
- Government documents
- Interlibrary loans of books
- Travel literature
- Miscellaneous pamphlets, including consumer information
- Telephone directories for major cities
- College catalogs
- Information on jobs, job hunting, and career development

Explore your college library to see what information resources are on hand—both for your research assignments and for your personal interests. Spend some time just browsing. There's no better way to get a feel for what's available and where to find it. Don't hesitate to check with a reference librarian, or other staff person, if you run into a problem.

The rest of this chapter will show you how to *use* information resources in preparing research papers. First, though, Skill Builder 8 provides a "painless" way of getting to know your college library.

Summary:
Exploring Your College Library

- **Scholarly books** are among the most important resources for college research. Both circulating books and reference books can be identified and located through card-based or electronic catalogs.
- **Periodicals** include newspapers, magazines, and scholarly journals. Journals are useful for many kinds of research and often provide more up-to-date information than books. Journal articles are identified and located through specialized indexes.
- **Reference materials** provide specific items of information without requiring large amounts of reading. While references such as encyclopedias can't be used as the *basis* for a research project, they can serve as a valuable supplement to scholarly books and journals.
- **Other resources,** both educational and recreational, are available in all college libraries. These resources may include reserve materials, nonprint materials and equipment, and popular books and periodicals. Some libraries offer access to computers and software.

Skill Builder 8:
Finding Information Resources

This Skill Builder will give you practice in identifying and locating information resources in your college library. Complete the Skill Builder at your library, using the Information Resources Worksheet on the next page.

INSTRUCTIONS

- Go to the section of the library that houses the microfiche or microfilm collection. If you're not familiar with these media or the reading machines required to use them, ask a staff person to help you. Then, *even if* old newspapers are available in printed form, use a reading machine to access a newspaper that was published on the day you were born. In the section of the Information Resources Worksheet headed "Birthday Newspaper," record the requested information about the newspaper you located.

- Then select a topic from the following list, or any other topic that you'd like to learn about.

Food Additives	Native Americans
Skydiving	Ballet
Personal computers	Dyslexia
Malcolm X	Plate tectonics
Dreams	Baseball
Electron microscopy	Pointillism

- Using the library's catalog, identify a book on your topic. Then go to the stacks and locate the book. Examine the book closely enough to complete the "Book Information" section of the worksheet.

- Use an appropriate index to identify a journal (or magazine) article on your topic. Then locate the correct issue of the periodical that you need. In that issue, read the article that you've identified. Fill in the "Periodical Information" section of the worksheet.

- When you've completed the worksheet, think back over what you've learned. Were you born on an important historical date? Did you find out something interesting about dreams? About Malcolm X? About plate tectonics? And last but not least: Was finding what you needed *really* as difficult as you expected?

Information Resources Worksheet

Birthday Newspaper

Title of newspaper ____________________

Volume number; publication date ____________________

Place of publication ____________________

Major front-page news story ____________________

____

____

Book Information

Title of book ____________________

Author(s) ____________________

Publisher ____________________

Publication date ____________________

Place of publication ____________________

Main point(s) of book ____________________ Call Number

____

____

____

____

Periodical Information

Title of article ____________________

Author(s) ____________________

Name of journal (or magazine) ____________________

Publisher ____________________

Volume number; publication date ____________________

Place of publication ____________________

Main point(s) of article ____________________

____

____

Page numbers of article ____________________

Using Information Resources Effectively

Exploring for information is an important early step in any research assignment. Next, though, you have to be able to *do* something with the information you gather. This section of the chapter will show you how. The section starts with general suggestions about the research process. Then, you'll learn some tips for using your information to write a research paper.

The Research Process

Research is a process, not an event. In assigning research papers, most college instructors allow students plenty of time to complete the work. In fact, it's not unusual for instructors to announce the due date of the research paper—along with the approximate date of the midterm exam—on the first day of class. There are at least three good reasons to start working on a research paper far in advance of the due date.

- First, it takes time to consider topics and decide on the best one. Topics selected late in the going rarely result in good papers—or good grades.
- Second, you have to "live with" your topic for quite a while before you can understand it fully. You should also live with each draft of your paper for several days or more so that you can be objective in evaluating and revising it.
- Third, by identifying resources and gathering information early you avoid the chance of discovering, at the last moment, that the materials you need have been checked out to other students.

Evaluating Your Information

Just because something appears in print doesn't always mean that it's completely accurate or that it represents the only way of viewing a particular topic. You need to be selective about which information you decide to keep and use. It's important to exercise your critical reasoning skills. That's one of the purposes instructors have in mind when they assign research papers. Here's a list of questions that you'll want to consider as you evaluate the information you find in books and journal articles.

- *Who is the author of the material?* Is he or she known for good scholarship in the area of your topic? Is he or she an expert in the field? To begin finding out, first check the author's qualifications. Most books and journals list authors' affiliations with colleges or other organizations. Often, authors' degrees, titles, or both are included.

  As you read books and articles, pay attention to the ways in which authors refer to each other's work. Make it a point to scan all reference lists and bibliographies included in the materials that you research. The authors and works cited most often are probably the main experts and "landmark studies" in the area of your topic.

  For more information about authors, you might check an edition of *Who's Who* or such specialized directories as *American Men and Women of Science* or *Contemporary Authors.*

- *Is the publisher reputable?* Major book publishing houses and professional groups that publish periodicals are likely to be more reputable than special-interest groups that advocate theories outside the scholarly mainstream. For example, a pamphlet or newsletter published by a group calling itself the Flat Earth Society probably would not be representative of modern scientific thought. Use your best critical judgment in evaluating special-interest materials.

- *Does the author seem objective?* You can develop a sense of authors' objectivity by reading a wide variety of books and articles on your topic. Also, think again about the authors' qualifications and affiliations. For instance, if you were doing research on health problems related to cigarette smoking, you probably could expect some differences in point of view between a journal article by a doctor and a position paper by a tobacco company official.
- *When was the material written?* Is it recent enough to include the latest findings in the area? Here again, reading a variety of books and articles can help you distinguish between out-of-date and current information on your topic.
- *Does the information agree with that from other sources?* If not, what are the main differences? Which sources seem more reliable? What factors might account for the differences? Above all, how will you go about reporting or resolving such differences in your paper? The best way to handle questions like these is to use enough resources to be sure that you've covered all main views of your topic.

Giving Credit

It's important to give credit to your sources of information when you write a research paper. Using someone else's work without acknowledging the source implies that the work is your own. This is called *plagiarism,* and it's a very serious offense. College penalties for plagiarism range from an "F" for the paper (or the course) to suspension from classes.

Of course, you don't have to give credit when you use information that's available in a number of resources. For example, the spelling of *Reykjavik,* the dates of the "Cuban Missile Crisis," and the molecular formula of benzene can be found in hundreds of reference books. Those aren't unique items of information. They don't "belong" to any particular author or publisher. Thus, you're not required to acknowledge your sources when you use information of that kind.

Here are three basic rules for acknowledging use of someone else's work.

- *Quoting.* Using a quotation can be a good way of making or supporting a point. When you quote someone else's work in a paper, always enclose the material in quotation marks and identify the source.
- *Paraphrasing.* Direct quotes aren't the only way to use other people's work in your papers. Sometimes it's quicker and just as effective to paraphrase—that is, restate—information from other sources. In such cases, although the wording is yours, the ideas are someone else's. Be sure to give proper credit to the author.
- *Integrating.* When you integrate material from two or more sources, your task is even more complex. Give credit to the authors, but make your own contribution clear. For instance, you might write: "Although Dr. X and Dr. Y seem to disagree, Dr. X was writing 20 years earlier than Dr. Y. Therefore, it is likely that Dr. Y's article took into account the more recent findings of . . . ."

Writing a Research Paper

Many college students, especially freshmen, have trouble writing research papers. With some students, the problem is poor writing skills. If that sounds like you, you owe it to yourself to get tutoring at once. The ability to express yourself well in writing is one that you'll benefit from time and again during college and beyond.

More often, the problem stems from the need to quickly *unlearn* the "research" methods often used in high school. Going to the library with an ill-defined topic and paraphrasing an encyclopedia article or pop-science best seller will not result in a successful college research paper. Nor will the practice of turning in a first draft written the night before the due date.

To do your best on college papers, you need to learn formal methods of conducting research and putting your findings on paper in an effective way. In addition, you need to know how to objectively evaluate and revise your work. Researching, writing, and revising papers will be easier if you break down the task into a series of steps.

1. Choose Your Topic Early

When an instructor assigns a research paper, listen carefully to be certain what kind of topic you can choose. Also, find out how long the paper should be and when it is due. Write down all of the requirements. Pay close attention to any handouts on the style or format to use in typing your paper. If your instructor recommends a particular style guide, get a copy as soon as possible.

Select a topic early and make sure it's one that interests you. Your research will be more stimulating—and you probably will achieve better results—when the topic is one that you really want to learn about.

If you sometimes have trouble coming up with ideas for research papers, it could be because you're trying too hard to arrive at a final topic at once. Many students find it helpful to start by developing a list of questions, issues, or problems that they would like to investigate. It's all right for your ideas to be rough at this early stage of research. Write down everything that occurs to you, as long as it's in keeping with the assignment.

Ideas can come from almost anywhere. Sources include class lectures and textbook readings, scholarly books and journals, newspapers and magazines, reference materials, television newscasts and documentaries, other students, and your own creative thinking.

Try out topics on your roommate or your classmates. By getting the reactions of your peers, you'll be able to narrow the list to the three or four topics that are best and most interesting. Also, other students' questions and comments about your topics can provide insights into how you could organize and present information in your paper.

Even if you feel confident of your ability to select a good topic, it's wise to check with your instructor early in your research. An ideal time for this would be after you've done enough thinking and reading to discuss options intelligently but *before* you've decided on your final topic. If your topic is too narrow, too broad, or not appropriate, your instructor can set you straight. In addition, if your topic is basically sound, but you've overlooked an important point, your instructor should be able to help you sharpen your focus. He or she might also suggest some authors, indexes, or specific publications with which to start your intensive research.

2. Identify Sources of Information

Write a brief statement defining the topic and purpose of your paper, including the main points that you want to make. Use this statement to help you think about how you'll organize your paper and what information you'll need. Then go to the library and begin identifying sources of information. Unless your instructor has stated otherwise, put most of your time and effort on identifying *scholarly books and journal articles* related to your topic. Scholarly books, remember, can be identified through the library's catalog; scholarly journal articles, through specialized indexes.

As you use the catalog and indexes, be sure to copy the titles, call numbers, and other information required to find your resources. When you're just starting out, copy the identifying information for *all* resources that seem likely to help you with your topic. Be as thorough as possible, even though you might (and probably should) make more passes through the catalog and indexes later. Don't be concerned about having too many resources. You'll probably find that some have been checked out to other students. Many more will prove to be out of date, not relevant, too basic, or too advanced.

If you have trouble using the catalog or indexes, or if you're not sure where to go for the materials you need, ask a library staff member for help.

3. Collect Information

When you're in the stacks and periodicals room locating your resources, inspect each book and article to get a better idea of whether it will contribute to your research.

For a book, skim the table of contents, the preface or introduction, the bibliography or reference list, and the index. Then read a few short samples of text to see whether the material is directly related to your topic. Also, make sure that the text is neither too basic nor too advanced. For a journal article, read the abstract (summary), then skim the introduction, conclusion, and bibliography or reference list. Read a few text samples, just as you would for a book.

With both books and journal articles, you'll want to use the resources whose textual content best helps you develop your topic. Once in a while, however, you may decide to use a resource simply because it has a good bibliography or reference list that provides leads to other materials.

As you select your books and articles, start digging out the information you'll need. If a book deals mainly with your topic, read the entire book. If a book deals with your topic only in passing, read the parts related to your topic and examine the rest closely enough to make sure that you're not missing anything important. Read all of your journal articles from beginning to end.

As you read your materials, take detailed and accurate notes. With general information—the kind that you might want to paraphrase in your paper—record the main ideas in your own words. When you find something that you think you might want to quote, copy it exactly. Put the material in quotation marks so you'll remember that the wording isn't yours.

Use ruled index cards or ruled writing paper for your notes. Record *only one* main idea, point, discussion, or "argument" on each index card or sheet of paper. This is important because later you'll sort, thin, and rearrange your notes to determine the best way of presenting the information in your paper.

On each card or sheet of notes, record all of the identifying information for the source that you've used. (When you're writing your paper, you'll need this information to prepare in-text acknowledgments and your bibliography or reference list.) For books, copy the full title (including any subtitle), the name(s) of the author(s), the name of the publishing house or group, the place and date of publication, and the page number(s) of the material you've taken notes on. Copy the same information for journal articles, but also include the title of the article and the name and volume number of the journal. Be sure to write down both the first and last page numbers of your article.

As an alternative to writing the source on each card or sheet of notes, you could compile a master list of sources. A master list should include complete identifying information for all of the sources that you've used. The sources should be numbered or lettered so that you can code each card or page of notes to the master list with brief entries like, for instance, "Source #16, p. 207." In this way, a master list of source materials can save you time and effort. The disadvantage is that, if you lose your master list, you'll have a lot of backtracking to do.

4. Organize Your Information

Read through your index cards or sheets of paper and sort your notes into categories. (If you've used a notebook or notepad, you'll need to separate the sheets now.) For example, all notes that might lend themselves to the introduction of your paper would become a category. Similarly, notes related to your likely main points would become other categories. Keep the notes for each category in a separate group.

When you've categorized all of your notes, arrange the groups in the order that shows the most logical flow of ideas. Then, within each group, arrange the individual cards or sheets. Experiment until you've found the sequence of ideas that would make the most sense to an objective reader of your paper. Remove material that no longer seems helpful. Leave in only the best of the information you've gathered.

Use your arranged notes to write an outline of your paper. Unless you have to hand in the outline to your instructor, don't fuss over the fine points of outline style. It's far more important for the *content* of your outline to be complete, accurate, and well organized. The outline, after all, is the framework on which you'll construct the first draft of your paper. Don't be tempted to skip the outline. The more thought and effort you put into it, the more smoothly your first draft will take shape.

If the outline shows that your topic is too broad, you'll need to scale the topic down. Outlining might also make it clear that you don't have enough information to support your topic or that your topic is too narrow. In that event, you'd need to return to the library to find more material on your topic or to get ideas for changing or expanding your topic. Don't forget that the bibliographies or reference lists in the first materials you read can help you to branch your research to other scholarly books and journal articles.

5. Write Your First Draft

With your outline as a guide, write the first draft of your paper. Write as quickly and naturally as you can. Refer to your notes when you need more detail than your outline provides. Try to get your ideas down in a fairly organized manner, but don't be too concerned about style or spelling yet. A good goal for the first draft is to think your topic onto paper from beginning to end, without getting stalled by little matters that can be fixed later.

Write in longhand, on a typewriter, or on a computer—whatever is easiest for you. Use double- or triple-spacing between lines so that you'll have room for revisions. Write on only one side of each page. This way, if your first draft is disorganized in places, you'll be able to cut it up and rearrange it.

One way to begin writing is by stating your topic as a question, issue, or problem. For instance, you might begin: "World War II had lasting and well known social, economic, and political effects on the United States. What is less well known, however, is the effect of World War II on that best loved of American conveniences, the automobile." Then, as you write, try to provide all of the information that a reader would need in order to fully understand and appreciate the topic you've stated.

Research papers often have four main sections.

- Introduction and description of the topic
- Discussion (the main body of information about the topic)
- Summary and conclusion
- Bibliography or reference list

Your instructor, or the recommended style guide, may suggest refinements to this basic structure. Within the appropriate structure, arrange your information in a sequence that would be easy to follow for a reader who is intelligent and informed but may not have much in-depth knowledge of your topic. Many kinds of material are best presented by combining a chronological approach with a "general to specific" approach.

As you write the first draft, don't wander from your stated topic; stick to the point. Include enough facts, examples, and other details to back up your ideas and to avoid being too general. Draw on the material that you've paraphrased from scholarly books and journal articles. Make careful, selective use of quotations. Don't feel that you must work in everything you've collected in your notes. Use only the material that most directly supports and advances your topic. Mark all paraphrased and quoted material. You can write the in-text acknowledgments either now or later when you've done your bibliography or reference list.

Remember that your paper must be more than just a rehashing of what the experts have to say about the topic. Although your research will have drawn heavily on the writings of others, the resulting paper must be *your work*. Be sure to include your own interpretations, findings, and conclusions.

6. Revise Your Draft

Set your first draft aside for a day or two. Then, go back and begin to evaluate and revise it. Don't assume that one revision will be enough. Plan on two or three rounds of revision, each dealing with a finer degree of detail.

For your first revision, reread the paper as objectively as you can. Be hard and honest in evaluating your work. Consider the paper as your instructor will. Have you selected a good balance of information resources and made the best use of them? Have you covered your topic completely and convincingly? Is the paper well organized? Does it move logically from one idea or section to the next? Have you stuck to the point? Are your facts and interpretations accurate? Is the length of the paper about right? Does the wording, although probably rough in places, seem approximately okay? Is the paper, on the whole, interesting and informative? Does it all make sense?

Before you start revising your first draft, you might want to show it to another student. The student doesn't have to know much about your topic. In fact, he or she doesn't even have to be taking the same course as you. The value of peer review is that other students generally can be counted on to give you honest editorial feedback about the organization, clarity, and interest level of your paper. A peer reviewer may or may not have the time and ability to suggest ways of improving your paper. Probably, though, your reviewer will be able to point out any major weaknesses that you've overlooked.

Make the corrections, changes, additions, and deletions needed to improve your paper. Focus on the "big picture" rather than on the small details. If the draft is poorly organized, cut it up and tape it back together in an order that presents the topic better.

Then read the draft aloud. If it sounds too rough, you'll need to devote as much attention to language as to content and organization. Slang and casual terms, of course, aren't appropriate in a research paper. You should try for a formal style, but you must avoid stilted writing. If your instructor has provided a handout or recommended a style guide, review the suggestions for writing your paper. Give some thought to your audience, too. Imagine you're writing not just for your instructor but for a group of informed readers that *includes* your instructor. What kind of writing would that audience expect?

7. Revise Your Draft at Least Once More

When your first revision has "cooled off" for a day or two, give it another reading. Again, evaluate the paper as your instructor will. Is it getting closer to a finished product?

If the content, organization, length, and language are acceptable, or nearly so, then on *this* round of revision you'll want to focus on a finer degree of detail. Matters that you might need to work on include the following.

- The title of your paper, if you haven't decided earlier
- Logical transitions between major sections of the paper
- Headings for the major sections
- Transitions between paragraphs within sections
- Grammar, spelling, punctuation, word choice, and tone
- In-text acknowledgments of your sources
- Bibliography or reference list

As you edit and polish this draft, you'll be equally concerned with what you're saying, how you're saying it, and how the material is formatted on the page. Try to get as close to a clean, finished draft as you can. You might want to call on your peer reviewer again, or another reviewer, especially if you sense that your paper "needs" something, but you are unable to identify the problem. Don't hesitate to put your paper through one or more *additional* rounds of revision, if that's what it takes for you to feel that you've done your best.

8. Prepare and Submit Your Final Draft

When you've made your last revisions and are satisfied with your paper, prepare your final draft. If you've been working on a typewriter or computer all along, the final draft should be mostly a cleanup of the previous one. If you've been writing longhand, you may need to switch to a typewriter or computer for your final draft. Many college instructors do not accept handwritten papers.

Select a good grade of 8½″ x 11″ white paper for your final draft. Use a black ribbon in your typewriter or computer printer and make sure the ribbon is fresh enough to provide dark, easy-to-read output. If you have a choice of type styles, don't get fancy. Choose one that's plain and highly readable—either in pica (10-pitch) size or elite (12-pitch) size.

Research papers usually are typed with double-spacing between lines and with generous margins all around. Other format requirements vary greatly, especially with regard to the title page or cover sheet, headings and subheadings, page numbers, and bibliography or reference list. Be sure to follow the requirements in your instructor's handout or the recommended style guide.

Work word-for-word from your previous revision. Make no new changes unless you spot a mistake or realize how something could be said more clearly. Above all, resist the urge to pad the wording of your paper. Last-minute additions of adjectives and adverbs rarely improve a paper and often detract.

When your final draft is finished, proofread it at least twice—ideally, on separate days. Make all corrections neatly. If a page has too many corrections, redo the entire page. Be sure that your name and any other required identification are on your paper in the proper place and format. When everything is in order, turn in your paper on time.

The worksheet in Skill Builder 9 can help you to evaluate and revise your college research papers. If you haven't written a paper yet, save the worksheet until you start your first one. If your first paper already has been graded and returned, use the worksheet to learn from the experience and to ensure better work on your next paper. Doing this can be especially helpful if, like many freshmen, you were disappointed with the grade that you received on your first paper.

Summary:
Using Information Resources Effectively

- One key to doing scholarly research in college is to start early so you'll have enough time to refine your topic and identify the best information resources.

  Other keys include evaluating information as you gather it and knowing when and how to acknowledge the use of other people's work.

- The process of researching, writing, and revising a successful college paper can be made manageable by dividing it into a series of steps.

  1. Choose Your Topic Early
  2. Identify Sources of Information
  3. Collect Information
  4. Organize Your Information
  5. Write Your First Draft
  6. Revise Your Draft
  7. Revise Your Draft at Least Once More
  8. Prepare and Submit Your Final Draft

Skill Builder 9:
Evaluating Your Research Papers

This Skill Builder will help you to identify strengths and weaknesses in your research papers at all stages of their development.

INSTRUCTIONS

- Select either a research paper that you're working on or a completed paper that recently has been graded and returned to you. (If you haven't yet done a college research paper, use this Skill Builder when you start your first one.)
- Read your paper objectively. Then answer the questions on the Research Paper Worksheet on the next page. For each question, circle "YES" if you believe your paper is satisfactory. Circle "NO" if you believe your paper is not satisfactory. Circle "?" if you're not sure.
- Total your responses in each column and think about your results. Were most of your circles in the "YES" column? What would you need to do in order to change your "NO" or "?" answers to "YES"? Do there seem to be any patterns among your "NO" or "?" answers? For instance, are most of your "NO" or "?" answers related to selecting and developing your topic? To organizing your paper? To language? To format or style?
- If you've used the worksheet with a returned paper, save both of them. As you plan, research, and write your next paper, refer to those documents to help you do better in any areas where you may have lost credit earlier.
- If you've used the worksheet with a paper that's in progress, revise the paper and correct any problems you've discovered. To cross-check your evaluation of your paper, ask another student to read and rate your paper, using one of the extra worksheets in Appendix A. (Leave one worksheet blank for making photocopies in the future.)

Research Paper Worksheet

YES	?	NO	**1.** Is your topic appropriate and relevant to the assignment?
YES	?	NO	**2.** Is your topic interesting and significant?
YES	?	NO	**3.** Is your topic focused as a question, issue, or problem?
YES	?	NO	**4.** Is your title accurate, concise, and effective?
YES	?	NO	**5.** Does your introduction capture the reader's attention?
YES	?	NO	**6.** Does your introduction clearly state the central idea?
YES	?	NO	**7.** Is your approach original and imaginative?
YES	?	NO	**8.** Is your choice of words precise and appropriate?
YES	?	NO	**9.** Are your sentences clear and effective?
YES	?	NO	**10.** Are your paragraphs unified and coherent?
YES	?	NO	**11.** Do your paragraphs follow one another logically and smoothly?
YES	?	NO	**12.** Are your ideas organized into a logical sequence?
YES	?	NO	**13.** Are your ideas supported with effective examples, quotations, etc.?
YES	?	NO	**14.** Is your presentation objective and unbiased?
YES	?	NO	**15.** Is your punctuation accurate and appropriate?
YES	?	NO	**16.** Is your spelling correct?
YES	?	NO	**17.** Is your capitalization correct and consistent?
YES	?	NO	**18.** Is your grammar correct and appropriate?
YES	?	NO	**19.** Are your sources fully and accurately identified?
YES	?	NO	**20.** Are your acknowledgments in proper form?
YES	?	NO	**21.** Are your page references correct?
YES	?	NO	**22.** Have you used quote marks for all direct quotations?
YES	?	NO	**23.** Is your bibliography or reference list complete, accurate, and in proper form?
YES	?	NO	**24.** Has your reading and observing been honestly reported?
YES	?	NO	**25.** Is your paper free of overused or repetitious words and phrases?
YES	?	NO	**26.** Is your paper free of slang and clichés?
YES	?	NO	**27.** Have your main points been summarized at the end?
YES	?	NO	**28.** Are your conclusions justified and appropriate?
YES	?	NO	**29.** Has your question, issue, or problem been effectively dealt with?
YES	?	NO	**30.** Has your paper been proofread for errors?
YES	?	NO	**31.** Are your pages numbered and do they have adequate margins?
YES	?	NO	**32.** Is your paper neat, clean, and legible?
___	___	___	
TOTALS			

Wrap-Up

This chapter has examined another of the study skills areas that require major adjustments of most college freshmen—understanding and using information resources.

In the first half of the chapter you saw that, while no college library can offer all possible information resources, most libraries have the basic resources that students need for their research projects and recreational uses. The main kinds of library information resources are scholarly books, periodicals (newspapers, magazines, scholarly journals), and reference materials—as well as other materials, equipment, and services to foster academic and personal growth among students.

You learned that scholarly books (identified through a print-based or electronic catalog) and scholarly journal articles (identified through specialized indexes) are the most appropriate sources of information for college research assignments. You then read some suggestions on how to use a library's catalog and indexes to identify and locate information for your research papers. Skill Builder 8 included a worksheet that can help you to start exploring and mastering the information resources of your college library.

The second half of the chapter took a look at ways of using information resources effectively. Research, as you saw, requires an early start so that your topic and your presentation of it can have time to mature. Another key to research is knowing how to evaluate the information you gather. It's equally important to know and observe the rules about giving credit to the sources you use.

You then read some suggestions for dividing the task of writing research papers into a series of easily managed steps. Here, again, an early start and adequate time are among your keys to success. You learned that it's crucial to evaluate and revise your paper at least twice before preparing the final draft. Skill Builder 9 provided a worksheet that you can use to improve your research papers.

Progress Check

Here's a chance for you to see how much you've learned about the information resources waiting for you in your college library. Match each of the definitions in the left-hand column with the appropriate information resource in the right-hand column. Write the correct letters in the blanks provided at the left.

____ **1.** A geographical dictionary	**A.** Library catalog
____ **2.** A system for looking up books by author, title, or subject	**B.** Atlas
____ **3.** A source of information about well-known people	**C.** Microfiche
____ **4.** A way of storing information from printed sources in a small amount of space	**D.** Gazetteer
____ **5.** A source of up-to-date statistics and general information about recent events	**E.** Index
____ **6.** A means of looking up articles in journals and other periodicals	**F.** Biographical directory
____ **7.** A book of maps and other geographical information	**G.** Almanac

---

The correct answers are: **1-D; 2-A; 3-F; 4-C; 5-G; 6-E; 7-B.** Did you get them all right? If not, you may want to review the section on "Exploring Your College Library."

Next Steps

In learning about the great variety of information resources available in college libraries, and ways of using those resources in conducting research, you've gained a powerful tool that can help you to learn more and get greater satisfaction from your college courses. This tool also can benefit you in the years following college.

Skill in using information resources, though, comes only with practice. If you haven't yet done your first college research paper, you probably will soon. You may be thinking about it—or *delaying* thinking about it—now. Whatever your situation, there's no time like the present for developing your skills to the level that will be necessary for success in college research assignments.

This chapter has gotten you off to a good start toward success and can serve as a valuable resource in the future. Refer to the chapter often as you work on your first few research papers. If you aren't familiar with your college library, begin exploring its information resources today. Check with library staff members and your instructors if you feel that you could use help in improving your research and writing skills.

Chapter 5

Preparing for and Taking Examinations

Warm-Up

Pop quizzes! Lab tests! Midterms! Finals!

By any name, examinations are vitally important to college students and can be sources of considerable pressure for many. In college courses, after all, it's not unusual for the midterm or final exam to cover weeks or months of material and to count as one-third to one-half of the grade for the term. That can be a big adjustment, particularly for college freshmen accustomed to preparing for and taking short, frequent tests in high school.

Many college freshmen quickly come to regard examinations as ordeals. As you might expect, they rarely do as well on exams as they could. Some fail to keep up with their readings, other assignments, and reviewing. As a major exam approaches, they find themselves too far behind to catch up. Some burn themselves out during exam week by abandoning their normal schedules for eating and sleeping. They skip meals, stay up late cramming, and sometimes pull all-nighters—largely because they don't realize that there's a better way to prepare themselves.

Others prepare themselves well enough but perform below their abilities on exams. They enter the exam room with a defeatist attitude. They misread directions or make other careless mistakes. They panic and forget material that they know. They fail to budget their time and set their priorities.

Now and then, you may experience one or more of these problems yourself. If so, this chapter can show you how to become more effective in preparing for exams and in taking them.

Overview and Benefits

The chapter begins with general exam preparation strategies and some tips on preparing for specific kinds of exams. Two Skill Builders are included so that you can begin to apply what you learn. The second major section of the chapter offers general suggestions for taking exams and ideas for taking specific kinds of exams. The section includes one Skill Builder.

Actually, all four of the previous chapters—Managing Time and Environment, Reading Textbooks, Taking Class Notes, and Using Information Resources—have included information helpful in preparing for and taking exams. For instance, if you keep up with assignments, set intermediate goals, get help when needed, and regularly review what you've learned, then you're preparing for the final exam every time you study. And when you do that, you've made a major breakthrough in your adjustment to the increased demands of college work.

Preparing for and taking exams are *skills* that, like all others, can be improved. No matter what your academic abilities are, you can develop your exam skills the same way that you would develop skills in chess, racquetball, cooking, or conversational Japanese—with time, effort, and practice. It can be hard work, but there are plenty of rewards.

- By making exam preparation a continuing, daily process, you'll reduce or eliminate the need for last-minute cramming.
- Because you'll have more confidence in your readiness for exams, you'll be able to control any feelings of "test anxiety."
- You'll avoid loss of credit caused by careless mistakes and, in general, will increase the likelihood of doing your best on exams.
- You'll master valuable life skills that may benefit you later in the workplace—for instance, in getting a job or in demonstrating your qualifications for a raise or promotion by means of an exam.

Checking Your Present Skills

The Self-Help Checklist that follows will get you started on analyzing your present skills, habits, and attitudes related to exam preparation and exam taking. Read each of the ten statements carefully and then mark your answer. Circle the letter "T" if the statement is *true* for you. Circle "F" if the statement is *false* for you.

Be honest with yourself. This checklist is for your use only. No one else need see your work. Mark the answers that accurately describe your approach to preparing for and taking exams—even if, in some cases, your answers differ from obviously "correct" ones. Be sure to respond to all ten statements.

Self-Help Checklist:
Preparing for and Taking Examinations

1. T F I often lose points on exams because of careless mistakes, even though I know the correct answers.

2. T F Before starting my final review for an exam, I make sure that I know exactly which lectures, textbook chapters, other readings, etc., will be covered.

3. T F When I finish an exam, I usually turn it in without checking it over.

4. T F Before starting to answer an essay question, I usually make a brief outline of the main points to cover.

5. T F When studying for an exam, I look through any previous exams in the course that have been graded and returned to me.

6. T F On an essay exam, I usually scan all of the questions before answering any of them.

7. T F When studying for an exam, I often make up practice questions and answer them in my own words.

8. T F I tend to take too long on the first parts of an exam and have to rush through the last parts.

9. T F In preparing for exams, I memorize information without fully understanding it.

10. T F I often study late, or even all night, just before a big exam.

- Statements 2, 4, 5, 6, and 7 are almost always *true* for students with good skills and habits in exam preparation and exam taking and positive attitudes about these processes.
- Statements 1, 3, 8, 9, and 10 are almost always *false* for students with good skills and habits in exam preparation and exam taking and positive attitudes about these processes.

What Do You Need to Work On?

The statements in the Self-Help Checklist are based on specific exam preparation and exam taking skills, habits, and attitudes that present problems for many college students. Look back over your answers to see how they compare with the key below the checklist.

As you do so, reread the ten statements. Ask yourself which of your exam-related skills, habits, or attitudes you need to devote the most attention to as you work through this chapter. The following pages can help you with all of the matters covered in the checklist—and quite a few more.

Preparing for Examinations

No examination can measure everything you know about a course or a subject area. Exams can only *sample* your knowledge. In any given course, your final exam will cover only a portion of the material that you were exposed to during the term. For some students, this presents difficulties in preparing for exams. They don't know what to study most carefully. Should they attempt to review everything covered in the course? Should they make some guesses and review only parts of the material covered? If so, *which* parts?

This section of the chapter presents techniques that can help you avoid uncertainties like those when you prepare for exams. By learning and applying these techniques, you can eliminate guesswork, study the right things the right way, and thus greatly increase your chances of doing well on examinations. You'll also find it easier to manage your anxiety about exams.

Preparing for All Examinations

Following are some general suggestions that can be helpful no matter what type of exam you're preparing for, from small lab tests to big midterms and finals. If you've read any of the four previous chapters, some of this material will have a familiar ring to it. Even so, the suggestions are worth considering again. Skill Builder 10 provides practice—and a reusable worksheet—for preparing for all types of exams.

1. Keep up With Assignments

The best way to simplify the task of preparing for exams is to keep up with the day-to-day assignments in your courses. Effective exam preparation begins on the first day of classes and continues throughout the term. If you haven't already done so, you need to plan a schedule that sets aside regular times for you to study new assignments and review previous ones. If you're having trouble finding enough time to keep up, you may want to turn back to Chapter 1, Managing Time and Environment, for some suggestions on scheduling study time. A good goal is to complete each reading assignment *before* it's discussed or lectured on in class. Never postpone your first reading of new material until just before an exam.

As you study each textbook assignment, carefully underline or highlight the most important points. Your textbook markings will help you to refresh your memory of the essentials when you review for an exam. Such markings are a necessity for college students. By exam time, you'll probably have been assigned far too much material for you to reread all of it.

Take organized notes in all of your courses. Many students find that comparing and cross-referencing their class notes with their reading assignments helps them acquire better understanding and recall of the subject matter.

When you have questions about material in a lecture, class discussion, or reading assignment, be sure to ask a reliable classmate or your instructor for help. Fully understanding today's work is essential for understanding tomorrow's.

2. Review Regularly

Research has shown that students remember academic material better when they review the material soon after their first exposure to it and frequently thereafter. If you really want to learn the subject matter, you can't leave reviewing until a night or two before an exam. You have to make reviewing a regular part of your study schedule.

Be sure that you're reviewing *actively,* however. Casually thumbing through previous notes and readings won't improve your knowledge of the subject matter. As you go over old material, ask yourself questions about it and answer them in your own words. The more often you quiz yourself as you review, the less you'll forget and the better you'll do when you're tested. In addition, regular review of old assignments usually makes new material in the course easier to understand.

3. Plan Ahead

When your instructor announces an examination, write down the date of the exam, the type of exam (e.g., objective, problem-solving, essay), the material to be covered, and the exam's "weight" in your grade for the course. Also write down any special rules about the exam—for instance, whether or not calculators will be allowed.

Keep track of upcoming exams on a calendar. Doing so will help you complete your readings or other assignments on time and get an early start on your final reviewing. Depending on the subject matter, length, and weight of an exam, you'll need to begin your final reviewing between several days and several *weeks* in advance. This way you'll have plenty of time to check with classmates or instructors if you find that you have trouble with any of the material. Schedule extra time for studying and reviewing topics that are especially difficult for you.

4. Identify What to Study

To study effectively for an exam, you must first identify what's important enough to study. If you've attended all classes, taken good notes, and reviewed them regularly, then you already have a start on determining what's important. Look for clues in your class notes. Where your instructor has repeated a topic or explained it in greater detail than others, it's probably important. Assume that you will be tested on all such material. Any material for which your instructor has prepared class handouts is also likely to appear on the exam.

Look for clues in your textbooks, too. Because review questions and exercises usually cover the most important content of a textbook chapter or other unit, they may indicate some of the topics likely to appear on an exam. Textbook headings, and your markings, can provide other clues.

Finally, look over any returned tests or exams in the course and, if they're available, your instructor's exams from the previous year. Earlier exams can provide clues to the kinds of questions that your instructor favors. If your instructor hasn't announced the proportions of lecture and textbook material to be on an exam, previous exams may give you a *rough* idea of what to expect.

5. Study Efficiently

Reviewing for a midterm or final exam may look like a huge task, but it can be managed if you begin early and work at it in stages. A good way to get started is by reviewing your class notes. First, look through your notes quickly, to refresh your memory of the main topics and how they relate to each other. Then, go over your notes more closely, to reacquaint yourself with the details and other supporting information. If you've taken good notes throughout the term, you'll find that they constitute *near*-complete summaries of each course.

It's unlikely that you'll have enough time to completely reread your textbook assignments. At a minimum, though, reread all chapter introductions and summaries and skim through all of the headings and subheadings as well as the material that you underlined or highlighted.

Compare your textbook assignments with your class notes and with any course outline or similar handouts. Some students find it helpful to prepare study outlines that tie together all of the main points covered both in their notes and in their textbooks. Simply *recopying* your notes, however, is not a good way to review because it doesn't require mental processing of the information.

When you've been over all of the material at least once and achieved a good overview, you can begin to focus on the topics you've identified as most likely to appear on the exam. Reread your class notes on all of these topics. Also reread all underlined or highlighted textbook material. Pay particular attention to major topics that appear both in the textbook and in your notes.

Then make up practice exam questions on the "most likely" topics. Where appropriate, write out the answers in your own words. Here and there, you might need to make yet another pass through your notes, your textbook, or both.

After you feel that you know the material, get together with some classmates and ask each other questions. You may find that you've overlooked one or more important topics. Make sure that this is really a study session, not a social get-together.

6. Learn to Manage Test Anxiety

Sweaty palms? Nervousness? Irritability? Sleeplessness? Lack of confidence? These are all symptoms of *test anxiety,* which, if severe, can hamper your performance on a test or exam—even when you know the material.

Test anxiety isn't all bad, however. A little anxiety can be a positive force. It can motivate you to study. It can encourage you to do your best in exam situations. A sensible goal, then, is not to eliminate test anxiety but to keep it at a healthy, productive level. The following tips can help.

- The best way to manage test anxiety is to prepare thoroughly for exams. When you feel confident that you know the material, it's much easier to stay calm under pressure.
- Practice your exam taking skills. Make up questions of the type (objective, problem-solving, or essay) that will be on the exam and try answering them. You may even want to conduct a full-scale rehearsal of the exam. To do this, you'll need to make up as many questions as you'll be tested on—and then complete them within the time limit that you'll be allowed on the exam itself. As an alternative to making up questions, you could use an exam that your instructor gave during the previous year, if "old" exams are available.

  The key here is to simulate real exam conditions as closely as possible. Time yourself, write out your answers, and rely on your memory rather than making use of your notes or books. You might even want to have your rehearsal in the room where the exam will be held. By giving you experience in performing under pressure, rehearsing can go a long way toward helping you keep anxiety in check during exams.

- Avoid last-minute review. If you're still studying some topics five minutes before an exam, you're likely to panic—and forget all the other material that you *do* know. Just before an exam, it's better to sit quietly and practice a relaxation technique such as deep breathing.
- Plan to review the material over a period of several days to several weeks before the exam. Then, on the night before the exam, do a light final review—and go to bed on time. Try to be so well prepared, so far in advance, that you could feel comfortable about going to a movie on the night before an exam.
- Don't upset your routine by staying up late (or all night) or getting up too early. Keeping to your regular schedule for sleep and meals will help you relax.
- If you try all of these suggestions and still feel overly anxious about exams, talk with one of the staff members at your academic advising office or campus counseling center.

7. **Review After the Exam**

Always review exams as soon as they are graded and returned to you. By making this a standard part of your exam preparation, you can gain valuable feedback in three important areas.

- How well you *know the subject matter* in each of your courses
- How well you *prepare for exams* in each course
- How well you *take exams* in each course

If scores or grades are posted but exam papers aren't returned, make an appointment to see your instructor during office hours to go over your exam.

Look for patterns among the questions that you missed, or lost points on, and try to figure out what caused your difficulties. Incorrect answers often indicate gaps in knowledge of the subject matter, but they might also suggest problems with exam preparation or exam taking.

Is one type of question usually hard for you? If so, that could point up weaknesses in your exam preparation skills, or exam taking skills, or both. For instance, if you frequently miss factual items, perhaps you need to devote more study time to learning specifics. If you lose a lot of points on essay questions, you may need practice in writing down your ideas quickly and logically under exam conditions. Your exam taking skills might also need strengthening if you make careless mistakes, accidentally skip questions, or run out of time before answering the final questions.

Other patterns may emerge if you consider matters like these in reviewing your exams.

- Did you miss more textbook material? Or more lecture material?
- Did you miss more material from the beginning of the course? Or more of the recent material?
- Did you miss more material early in the exam? Or more material late in the exam?

For each question that you missed, or lost points on, determine exactly what went wrong.

- Failed to read (understand, remember, follow) directions?
- Misread questions?
- Knew information but made mistakes in responding to questions?
- Committed other oversights or careless errors?
- Became too nervous or anxious to concentrate?
- Ran out of time?
- Didn't realize the material was to be covered on the exam?
- Realized the material was to be covered but either didn't review it or didn't learn it well enough?
- Knew the material well but couldn't fully recall it when needed?

Take immediate action on any problems that you identify in reviewing returned exams. When you've missed questions, write them down at the appropriate places in your class notes. Then review your notes, textbook, and any other materials to determine the correct answers. Write these down, too—along with your findings as to why you missed the questions. If you made up practice questions before the exam, check to see how close they were to the "real" ones you were tested on. Keep the exam in your notebook for future reference.

If there's a topic or procedure that you still don't understand, get help from a reliable classmate or from your instructor. Don't assume that, because the exam is over, it's no longer important. The material could be the basis for everything else you'll be expected to learn during the rest of the course or in an advanced course later.

Summary:
Preparing for All Examinations

1. Keep up with day-to-day assignments so as to simplify reviewing later for exams.
2. Review your class notes and reading assignments regularly to improve your understanding and recall of the material on exams.
3. Plan ahead and begin your final reviewing several days to several weeks before the exam.
4. Identify what to study by reviewing your class notes and handouts to see which topics the instructor has emphasized most. Look for other clues in your textbooks and in earlier exams.
5. Study efficiently by focusing on the topics you've identified as most likely to be on the exam and answering questions about them in your own words.
6. Keep test anxiety at a manageable level by preparing thoroughly, practicing your exam taking skills, and avoiding last-minute cramming.
7. Review returned exams to learn from any mistakes you may have made.

Skill Builder 10:
Preparing for Examinations

In this Skill Builder you'll practice a series of steps that can help you prepare effectively for all kinds of examinations. Use the procedure described here to prepare for an upcoming exam in one of your courses.

INSTRUCTIONS

- Think of a test or exam that has been announced for one of your courses. In item 1 ("Exam Information") of the Exam Preparation Worksheet on the next page, write down what you know about the exam.
- Review the exam information that you recorded in item 1. As you do so, think about the assigned study activities that you'll need to complete before you begin reviewing for the exam.
- In item 2 on the worksheet, list the study activities that you need to complete. Spread out your remaining studying over a period of several days to several weeks and set realistic deadlines for completing the activities. Try to schedule the work so that you'll finish all of your assignments well before the exam and still have plenty of time for reviewing. Check off each study activity as you complete it.
- In item 3, schedule the review activities that you'll need to do (after completing all of your assignments) in order to be fully prepared for the exam. To avoid last-minute cramming, spread out your reviewing over several days or more. Set a realistic deadline for each review activity. Check off the activities as you complete them.

If you find this procedure helpful and would like to continue following it, use the extra Exam Preparation Worksheets in Appendix A. Leave one worksheet blank for making photocopies.

Exam Preparation Worksheet

1. Exam Information

Course name and section ________________

Day, date, time, and place of exam ________________

Kind of exam ___ Essay ___ Multiple-choice ___ True-false
___ Short answer ___ Problem-solving ___ Other

Amount of time allowed for exam ________________

"Weight" of exam in total grade for course (if known) ________ %

Textbook chapter(s) or pages covered on exam ________________

____

____

Lecture or discussion topics covered on exam ________________

____

____

Other material or activities covered on exam (films or videotapes, lab experiments or demonstrations, etc.) ________________

____

2. Study Completion Schedule

STUDY ACTIVITY	DEADLINE
Textbook chapter(s) or pages to read ________ ________________	________
Lecture or discussion notes to correct, expand, or (if missing) copy from a classmate ________ ________________	________
Other materials or activities to finish ________ ________________	________

3. Review Schedule

REVIEW ACTIVITY	DEADLINE
Review textbook chapter(s) or pages	________
Review lecture or discussion notes	________
Compare textbook material with class notes	________
Review other materials or activities	________
Review with small group of other students (optional)	________

Preparing for Specific Kinds of Examinations

The preparation skills that were presented in the previous section can be valuable no matter what type of exam you're getting ready for. There are other techniques that are helpful for specific types of exams. This section describes some effective ways of preparing for objective, problem-solving, and essay exams.

In college, as in high school, you'll sometimes be asked to recall and paraphrase information you've learned and to recognize correct answers among incorrect alternatives. More typically, though, you'll be asked to reason things out and *apply* what you've learned to new situations that differ from those discussed in class and in your textbooks. For many freshmen, this can be another of the major adjustments required to succeed in college. The suggestions that follow can help you make that adjustment.

Objective Examinations

Common types of objective examinations include multiple-choice, true-false, fill-in-the-blanks, and matching. The first of these—multiple-choice—is the kind of objective exam most frequently given in college. If you haven't yet had objective exams in college, you may soon discover that they resemble objective tests in high school only in their appearance. In terms of *what* they test and *how* they require you to demonstrate your knowledge of the subject matter, they may be very different from the objective tests you were given in high school.

For instance, if you were studying the Panama Canal in high school, a multiple-choice question might ask you to pick the year of the canal's completion from among four or five possibilities. In college, though, a multiple-choice question on the Panama Canal would probably require you to demonstrate greater understanding of the subject matter. A possible question might be: "If the United States had not intervened to ensure completion of the Panama Canal, which of the following consequences would have been most likely during World War II?"

Questions like the latter require you to demonstrate your abilities to reason and to apply your knowledge to new situations. You may associate reasoning and application with essay exams, but, in college, you're just as likely to have to demonstrate these abilities on objective exams. So, when you study for an objective exam, you'll need to know the main ideas just as thoroughly as you would for an essay exam. By making sure that you have the "big picture" first, you'll find it much easier to learn the numerous facts and other details that you'll need to know.

To prepare for factual items, focus on *important* information. Don't try to memorize the entire textbook. What's important? Probably only the facts and other specifics that *directly* relate to or support the main ideas or topics of the course. The small details in a textbook chapter or lecture rarely will be worth your time.

You may find it helpful to write out lists of dates, definitions, formulas and equations, and so forth. For instance, if you're reviewing French vocabulary, a list could be a very effective study aid. You might want to list French words in one column and their English meanings in another.

Be sure to vary the ways in which you run through the list so your ability to recall the material won't be limited to a certain order. If you've been reading the list from top to bottom, be sure to read it from bottom to top—or in some other order—several times. If you've been looking at the French words and trying to remember the English, reverse the procedure once or twice. Although you're studying for an objective exam, your goal isn't just to memorize information but to understand it thoroughly.

Some students use memory aids to help them remember facts for objective exams. Memory aids can be helpful, but don't make up such complex ones that they become more difficult to remember than the material you needed to learn in the first place. Also, to avoid confusion, it's wise not to make up too many such aids for a single topic or exam.

After you have reviewed carefully, both for the big picture and for the factual items that you expect, ask a friend to quiz you. If the practice questions reveal any general topics or specifics that you're not well prepared for, go over that material in your notes and textbook again.

Problem-Solving Examinations

Problem-solving examinations typically involve using a formula or applying a rule in a step-by-step process that may require computation. They're most often given in math and natural science courses. You might also encounter problem-solving exams if you take economics, accounting, or computer science.

The best way to prepare for problem-solving exams is to learn and understand key theorems, rules, formulas, and equations—there's the big picture again—and then practice applying them to a variety of problems similar to those you will be tested on. As you review your notes, pay particular attention to the kinds of problems that your instructor worked or discussed in class.

Your textbook may include practice problems. If so, work all of the problems available. Be sure to check your work; there's no point in practicing incorrect procedures. Don't look at the answer key too soon, though. To make sure that you really understand the principles involved, try to solve each problem all the way through, on your own. That's exactly what you'll have to do when you're tested on the material.

Finally, make up some practice problems. Ask your friends to make up problems, too. Then exchange your problems with one another, work the problems, and talk about the procedures you used to find the solutions. If you need more practice, check with your instructor or a reference librarian. They may have other textbooks in which you can find problems of the kind that you need to work on.

Essay Examinations

Essay examinations are very challenging for many college freshmen because they call on skills not widely taught or tested in high school. These are the skills that enable you to interpret, organize, and apply in written form the information you have learned. For instance, an essay test in college may ask you to compare the foreign policies of two presidents or to design a procedure for carrying out a psychological experiment.

Like objective and problem-solving examinations, essay exams require you first to master the big picture. The means of demonstrating your knowledge of the big picture is quite different, however, on essay exams. You'll be expected to write well reasoned, well organized answers of moderate to considerable length.

To prepare for essay exams in college, concentrate on interpreting and applying the main ideas and topics you've learned. For instance, if you've been studying the Bill of Rights, you could spend some time thinking about how your life might be different without its protection. You'll still need to know the facts—too general an answer won't be acceptable—but you'll also need to know the implications of the facts.

Reviewing your notes on lectures and class discussions can help you here. Look for the main ideas and topics in your notes, especially those that your instructor emphasized. Put extra effort on any topics that your instructor hinted might be on the exam. Also, review your textbook. Often, textbook topic headings can provide clues about the questions to expect on an essay exam.

When you're confident that you know the basic information in your textbook and notes, start making up practice questions. Think about whether certain topics lend themselves to particular types of essay questions—for instance, "compare and contrast," "refute or defend," "trace the development of," and so forth. If Chapter 11 was about the Korean Conflict and Chapter 12 about the U.S.-Soviet "Cold War," think of questions that focus on the similarities and differences of the two situations.

Try writing your answers on paper and checking them against your textbook and notes. Are your answers complete and accurate? Are they well organized? Do they make sense? Again, you may want to exchange sample questions with friends and compare answers. Group sessions can be useful both for answering likely essay questions and for identifying others that you might not have considered.

Skill Builder 11 will help you practice preparing for essay exams.

Summary:
Preparing for Specific Kinds of Examinations

- For **objective exams** learn the big picture and the important dates, facts, and other details.
- For **problem-solving exams** learn the big picture and practice applying key theorems, formulas, and equations on a variety of problems.
- For **essay exams** learn the big picture and practice answering questions about the main topics in your own words.

Skill Builder 11:
Preparing for Essay Examinations

This Skill Builder will help you improve your ability to identify, and prepare for, possible essay questions in your textbook reading assignments. Use the procedure described here to help you prepare for your next essay exam.

INSTRUCTIONS

- Choose a chapter or other passage that you've been assigned to read in one of your textbooks. Read the material carefully. As you do so, mark topics that you think your instructor might consider important enough to ask questions about on an essay exam.
- When you've finished reading the textbook assignment, review the topics that you marked. For each of those topics, think of the kind of essay question that your instructor might ask on an exam. Write the first of your questions in the appropriate blanks on the Essay Exam Worksheet that follows. Also record the source of your question—for instance, "text, pp. 308-313."
- Write the rest of your questions on the extra worksheets included in Appendix A. (Make photocopies of the worksheet, if necessary. Leave one worksheet blank for making additional photocopies in the future.) Write only one question on each worksheet. Number your worksheets in order, if you wish.
- Now take your essay exam yourself, using the remaining blanks on the worksheets for answering your questions. Give yourself a realistic time limit—about the same amount of time that your instructor would allow for a real exam.
    - For each question, first quickly jot down the key facts and ideas that you'll need to include in your answer. Then number the facts and ideas to form a brief, logical outline.

- Following your outline, write out the answer to each question, in your own words. Cover the topic thoroughly but don't "pad" your answer.
- Before your time limit is up, take two or three minutes to check your work. Read your answers for completeness and correctness—both of content and of such matters as spelling, punctuation, and grammar. Correct any errors or omissions.

■ Finally, check each of your answers against the textbook assignment. Correct and improve your answers as necessary. You may find it helpful to make your corrections with a color pen or marker, to highlight areas where your preparation skills for essay exams need further strengthening.

No. ____ of ____

Essay Exam Worksheet

Essay Question and Source: ______________________________

____

____

____

Answer: ______________________________

____

____

____

____

____

____

____

____

____

____

____

____

____

____

____

____

____

____

____

____

____

____

____

____

____

Taking Examinations

Developing good examination taking skills is especially important if you're new on the college campus. In college, unlike high school, your grade in a course may be based on only two or three exams and a paper. Doing less than you're capable of on any of these could lower your course grade for the whole term.

Another reason to polish up your skills is that exams are common in the workplace—to get a job, to keep a job, to obtain a certificate or license, to show your qualifications for a raise or a promotion. Being able to demonstrate what you know or can do in a testing situation is an important life skill for many people.

Some of the tips presented in this section of the chapter, like monitoring your time and checking your work, apply to all exams. Other tips apply to certain kinds of exams. Obviously, you would respond in different ways to an essay exam in sociology and a problem-solving exam in calculus. As you go through the following material, give extra attention to the tips for the kinds of exams that are hardest for you.

General Tips for Taking Examinations

No matter what kind of examination you have coming up next, there are some tried-and-true general strategies that can increase your chances of doing your best work. These strategies are most effective when you've made a serious, consistent effort to prepare yourself academically. The so-called "test-wise" tricks that you may sometimes hear about from other students will *not* be covered. "When in doubt, pick 'C'"? Forget it; that's bad advice. Besides, with solid academic preparation and the tips in this chapter, you'll have no need for such desperate measures.

1. Get Under Control

You've kept up with your studies throughout the term. You've reviewed thoroughly and quizzed yourself with a variety of practice questions. Now the only remaining thing you need to do to ensure your best performance on the exam is to get yourself under control as the time approaches.

Being under control includes, among other things, having a good night's sleep before the exam and eating your meals at their regular times. It also includes arriving at the examination room five or ten minutes early so you can pick a seat (if that's allowed) and focus your thoughts on working very hard for the full time available.

In addition, being under control means making sure that you've brought all of the supplies or materials that you need. Many students realize just as an exam is beginning that they've forgotten to bring pencils or pens, a calculator, or some other necessary item. When you go to an exam, take everything you'll need, including *extra* pencils or pens. Also, take a watch so you can keep track of your time.

It's probably best not to discuss the exam with your friends when you arrive at the examination room. If someone mentions a topic that you overlooked, you might start worrying and have trouble recalling the material that you *did* study.

2. Follow Directions

Before starting an exam, clear your mind of distracting thoughts and read all the directions carefully, both those on the exam paper and any on the chalkboard. If your instructor gives oral directions, listen carefully. Make certain that you understand what you are required to do. For instance, when the directions on an essay exam are to "Answer any three of the following five questions," you'll waste time and lose valuable points if you write five sketchy answers instead of three well developed ones. When you read exam directions, you may find it helpful to underline or highlight such key conditions as (in the preceding example) "Answer any three . . . ."

If the directions for the exam or for a particular section or question seem unclear to you, don't guess at their meaning. Ask your instructor.

3. Plan Your Time

Before you begin an exam, plan how you'll use your time. Quickly skim the entire exam—both the directions and the questions—and plan your time according to the number, type, and point value of the questions. Generally, the amount of time you spend on a question should be related to its point value. Your plan should, of course, allow time to answer all of the questions. It should also include a few minutes at the end of the exam for a quick review of your work. As noted previously, it's a good idea to take a watch to exams so that you can pace yourself.

4. Start With What You Know Best

When you've looked over the exam and planned how to use your time, begin with the section or the specific questions that you know best and feel most comfortable with. While this is a good strategy for any kind of examination, it's most helpful for problem-solving exams and essay exams, where students often have trouble getting started.

This approach to starting an exam offers at least three major advantages.

- It ensures that you'll get full credit for the material you've learned best.
- As you work on questions that you know, you'll gain confidence and find it easier to keep test anxiety in check.
- While you're working on the easier questions, the information you'll need to answer the more difficult ones may begin to come to you.

5. Read Thoroughly

Read each question carefully and completely before you answer. Make sure you understand exactly what the question asks and what you are to do in answering it. Underline or highlight key words in questions just as you would in the directions. Reread questions that are confusing.

If, after rereading a question, you have no idea how to answer it, put a mark next to it and move on to the next question at once. Go back to the unanswered questions when you've completed the rest of the exam.

6. Don't Rush

Don't be concerned if other students finish before you do. Your instructors will be more impressed by thoroughness than by speed. Use all of the time allowed so that you can do your very best on the exam. Work quickly, but don't rush. Hurrying can lead to omissions, miscalculations, and other careless errors. Also, you're much more likely to tense up and forget information if you're feeling rushed.

7. Have a Panic Strategy

When you're under pressure during an exam, it's easy to get disturbed by a question that you aren't prepared for or by a passing memory lapse. For many students, the tendency at such times is to panic. Mild levels of anxiety, as you've learned, can help students perform well on exams. Panic, however, detracts from performance by causing students to become confused, discouraged, and unable to remember the material that they've learned. For this reason, it's a good idea to have a way of dealing with the panic that may arise in a testing situation.

One good panic strategy is to give yourself a brief time-out if you ever start to "lose it" during an exam. Put the exam temporarily out of mind. If you're allowed to leave the room, it might be enough to take a quick walk to the nearest water fountain.

Of course, you don't have to leave your desk or chair. You can take a time-out right where you are. To do so, just take slow, deep breaths and let yourself relax for a moment. Close your eyes if you want to. Picture yourself confidently resuming work, turning in a completed exam, and leaving the room with a good feeling of having done your best work. Allow 20 to 30 seconds for your time-out. That's probably all you'll need to get your panic under control and start back to work on the exam.

8. Check Your Work

Use the last few minutes of the exam period to check, edit, and proofread your work. Look for omitted and mismarked answers, miscalculations, spelling and grammatical errors, and other careless mistakes. Correcting several small oversights might raise your score by a whole letter-grade. Don't forget to put your name, and any other required identifying information, on your exam paper.

Summary:
General Tips for Taking Examinations

1. Get yourself under control as the time for an exam approaches. Arrive early and make sure you've brought all needed supplies and materials.
2. Make certain that you understand the directions for an exam before you begin. If you are unsure about the directions, ask your instructor to explain.
3. Plan how you'll use your time during the exam. Pace yourself so you'll have enough time to answer all questions and review your work.
4. To build your confidence, start with the questions that you know best and feel most comfortable with.
5. Read each question carefully and completely before giving your answer. Make sure your answer responds directly to what the question asks.
6. To avoid tensing up and making careless mistakes, work quickly but don't rush. Use all of the time allowed.
7. Have a strategy for regaining confidence and control in case you start to panic during an exam.
8. Allow a few minutes at the end of the exam to check, edit, and proofread your answers.

Tips for Taking Different Kinds of Examinations

The most common types of examinations in college are objective, problem-solving, and essay. This section presents specific tips for doing your best on each of these kinds of exams.

OBJECTIVE EXAMINATIONS

Objective exams vary greatly in question format and scoring method. At many colleges, multiple-choice exams are the most common kind of objective exams. The following tips can help you do your best on multiple-choice and other objective exams.

1. Respond to All Questions

Answer all questions. If they're all of the same type, answer them in order. If there are several types or sections of questions, start with the type or section that you feel most comfortable with. Don't spend too long on any one question. When you're unsure of your answer to a question, or you can't answer at all, put a mark beside the question. If time permits, go back to such questions after you've answered all the others.

2. Read All Answer Choices

On multiple-choice exams, read all of the answers for each question before making your choice. To test for in-depth knowledge, instructors often include answer choices that seem plausible but either aren't quite correct or aren't the *best* answers provided. Even though the first answer choice may appeal to you, the correct or best answer may be farther down the list.

3. Watch Subtleties of Wording

Read carefully for qualifying words such as "not," "least," and "except" that are easy to miss if you're just skimming questions. Often, an instructor will make these words stand out through the use of underlining, capital letters, or boldface type, but you can't assume that will always be the case. It's important to detect and understand all such qualifiers. If you overlook one, your answer to the question will be wrong because you'll have used a logical process exactly the opposite of what's required.

Also, pay close attention to any adjectives, adverbs, or other modifiers in objective questions. Modifiers (and other words) that are *extreme* or *absolute*—for instance, "always" or "never," "all" or "none"—often make an answer choice incorrect. Be careful, though. There's no firm rule about such words.

Being alert to subtleties of wording is an important exam taking skill. On multiple-choice exams, for instance, this skill may save you time in eliminating some incorrect answer choices. However, it's no substitute for thorough knowledge of the subject matter, and it won't enable you to do well on an exam if you haven't studied.

4. Watch for Multiple Concepts

Watch for multiple ideas or concepts within the same statement. All parts of a statement must be correct or the entire statement is incorrect. For example, consider the statement, "Cubism is exemplified by some of the early twentieth-century paintings of Braque, Gris, Modigliani, and Picasso." If that were a true-false question, the correct answer would have to be "False" because Modigliani was not a Cubist.

What if the same information were presented in a multiple-choice question? In that case, a statement like "Cubism is exemplified by some of the early twentieth-century paintings of:" might begin the question. If one of the answer choices were "Braque, Gris, Modigliani, and Picasso," you could immediately rule out that choice because part of it ("Modigliani") is incorrect.

5. Check Your Work

Set aside a few minutes at the end of the exam to check your work. Look for omitted answers, mismarked answers, and other careless mistakes. If there are too many questions for you to check all of your answers, check those that you feel uncertain about. If there's no "penalty" or scoring correction for wrong answers, it's to your advantage to make a guess at any questions that you didn't answer earlier. Be sure that you know what the directions say about guessing.

On tests that will be scored by machine, make certain that you've followed the directions on how to "grid in" your answers, name, and other identifying information. Erase any stray marks that you've made.

PROBLEM-SOLVING EXAMINATIONS

Problem-solving examinations usually consist of mathematical, scientific, or business-related problems to be worked by using a formula or applying a rule, often in a step-by-step process that involves computation. Here, it is most important that you minimize careless mistakes by checking your calculations, the placement of decimal points, and so forth. The following tips should help.

1. Make Notes

Write down, on your exam paper, all hard-to-remember formulas, equations, rules, etc., as soon as the exam begins but before you start working the problems. If you have a memory lapse during the exam, a quick look at your notes may provide the information that you need.

2. Work the Easiest Problems First

Earlier you learned that, unless there's a particular reason for doing exam questions in order from start to finish, it's a good idea to begin with those that you know best and find easiest. On problem-solving exams, this approach can help you get off to a fast start and gain confidence in your ability to work the remaining problems.

3. Work Problems One Step at a Time

Don't get frustrated and, above all, don't give up if you can't immediately work through to the answer of a problem. Work one step at a time. Often, completing one step of a problem will help you remember or figure out what the next step should be.

4. Do All That You Can

If a problem is hard, but you have a general idea of the process involved, do all that you can to work the problem. Write down your best answer and be sure to show all of your work. Even if your answer is incorrect, you may get partial credit if you have used the right process.

If you are *completely* unable to work a problem, don't waste time on it. Move quickly on to the next one and come back later if time permits. By then you may have remembered how to work the problem that stumped you earlier. Also, you might have picked up clues from some of the other problems.

5. Be Organized

Show all of the steps in your work and clearly identify or label your answer so that your instructor can find it quickly. Make sure that everything you put down is neat enough to be read and understood at a glance.

6. Check Your Work

Whenever possible, check all answers in a different way from that used when you first did the work. For example, add *up* a column of figures when checking if you added *down* the column when you first solved the problem.

ESSAY EXAMINATIONS

Questions on essay exams may ask you to "discuss the causes," "compare the outcomes," or "give examples" in regard to specified topics. Skill Builder 12 provides practice in recognizing the meanings of some terms that are commonly used in essay questions.

In answering essay questions, stick to the topic. Use the points assigned to each question as an approximate guide to the amount of information that your instructor expects. For instance, if you have a three-question test with one question worth 60 points and the other two worth 20 points each, you should not plan to spend an equal amount of time on each question.

The following tips can help you to do your best on essay examinations.

1. Read All Questions Before Beginning

Quickly read through all of the questions before answering any of them. As you do so, notice the number of points assigned to each question and divide your time accordingly. Also, jot down beside each question any relevant facts or ideas that occur to you. This overview of the exam will help you budget your time and avoid overlapping answers.

2. Answer the Easiest Questions First

Begin with the questions that you know best and find easiest. This will help you feel more confident and will also serve as a good warm-up for the more difficult questions ahead. Don't spend too long on easy questions, though. If the instructor intended them to be easier than other questions, they're probably worth fewer points.

3. Concentrate on One Question at a Time

Trying to think of your answer to Question 2 while writing the answer to Question 1 will only confuse you. Focus on one question at a time, write the best answer you can, then move on to the next question.

4. Understand the Questions

Decide what kind of answer each question requires before you begin writing. Make sure that you know exactly what you are to do. This will be made clear by the main verb in the question. Different kinds of responses are required by different verbs. "Compare," "define," "describe," "discuss," "explain," "identify," "illustrate," and "list" are among the verbs you can expect to encounter on essay exams.

5. Make an Outline

To ensure good organization and to prevent repetition and omissions, make a short outline for each answer before you start writing. It shouldn't be an elaborate outline. Just list the key points to be covered, each expressed in a brief phrase. Then quickly number the points in logical order.

Because of the time limit, you needn't be too concerned about trying to achieve an "elegant" writing style in your answers. However, your spelling, punctuation, and grammar have to be correct and your thoughts must be well organized. Starting with an outline will ensure that your answers stay on track.

6. Get to the Point

Avoid writing long-winded introductions and going off on tangents. Your aim in answering essay questions is to record the largest amount of *relevant, point-earning* information in the time allowed. Needless wording won't help your score and only wastes your time. Later, it wastes your instructor's grading time and may cause him or her to become annoyed with you.

A brief, to-the-point topic sentence should introduce each answer. For example, you might begin, "There were four main reasons why the United States became militarily involved in Vietnam." Then move right into the topic, stating each of your points in order. Develop each point fully, but don't "pad" your answer.

7. Include Specifics

When appropriate, include facts, examples, analogies, and other specifics to support your answers. Facts show your instructor that you know the material in detail. Examples and analogies show that you understand how the material is related to other topics.

8. Be Neat

Write legibly and make any corrections as neatly as possible. Most instructors react favorably to neatness, so let this work to your advantage. Besides, if your writing is unreadable, you'll find that few instructors will spend time on deciphering it.

Use a separate paragraph for each main idea. This helps the instructor follow your reasoning.

9. Allow Room to Expand

Leave space between your answers. You may need it for new ideas or additional details that occur to you later when you reread what you have written.

10. Check Your Work

Leave enough time to check all your answers for organization, for completeness and accuracy of content, and for correctness of grammar, spelling, and punctuation. As you do so, quickly reread each question. If there are any multipart questions, make sure you've answered all of the parts. You might raise your score by fixing a few such errors or oversights.

Summary:
Tips for Taking Different Kinds of Examinations

OBJECTIVE EXAMINATIONS

1. Respond to all questions.
2. Read all answer choices.
3. Watch subtleties of wording.
4. Watch for multiple concepts.
5. Check your work.

PROBLEM-SOLVING EXAMINATIONS

1. Make notes.
2. Work the easiest problems first.
3. Work problems one step at a time.
4. Do all that you can.
5. Be organized.
6. Check your work.

ESSAY EXAMINATIONS

1. Read all questions before beginning.
2. Answer the easiest questions first.
3. Concentrate on one question at a time.
4. Understand the questions.
5. Make an outline.
6. Get to the point.
7. Include specifics.
8. Be neat.
9. Allow room to expand.
10. Check your work.

Skill Builder 12:
Understanding Key Verbs in Essay Questions

This Skill Builder will help you improve your ability to recognize and respond to some of the key verbs that are used in essay questions.

INSTRUCTIONS

- Scan the material on the Key Verbs Worksheet on the next page. In the left-hand column is a list of verbs that you're likely to encounter on essay exams. In the right-hand column, in scrambled order, are the meanings of the verbs.
- Match the verbs with their meanings. Use the blank to the left of each verb (or group of verbs) to write in the letter of the correct meaning. When you've finished, check your work against the answer key in Appendix B.
- After you've checked your answers, start applying your knowledge. Pick a course in which you expect to have an essay exam. Think of a good essay question for each of the nine verbs (and groups of verbs) on the worksheet. Base your questions on the content of your reading assignments *and* all related class lectures and discussions.
- Write your essay questions in your notebook for the course, or use extra copies of the Essay Exam Worksheet (from Skill Builder 11) that's included in Appendix A.
- Then write out complete answers to your questions. Check your answers against the textbook and your class notes. This procedure will sharpen your skills both in predicting and in answering likely essay questions. Later, when you prepare for an actual examination, review your practice questions and answers. Try to improve them, using the suggestions in this chapter.

Key Verbs Worksheet

____ **1.** Compare

____ **2.** Contrast

____ **3.** Criticize or Evaluate

____ **4.** Define

____ **5.** Describe, Discuss, or Explain

____ **6.** Illustrate

____ **7.** List, Outline, or Summarize

____ **8.** Prove

____ **9.** Trace

A. Briefly state main points, facts, ideas, or concepts

B. State the meaning of a word or concept

C. State the differences between or among things, ideas, events, or problems

D. Demonstrate that something is true by giving factual evidence or logical reasons

E. Use analogies or examples to tell about or clarify a point or problem

F. State the similarities between or among things, ideas, events, or problems

G. State the progress, development, or history of something in chronological order

H. Give a complete, balanced overview of a topic, with details

I. State your view or opinion on a subject, giving facts or reasons

Wrap-Up

In this chapter, you've seen that effectiveness in preparing for and taking college examinations isn't a natural talent that some students have and other students lack. It's an acquired *skill* that every student can develop and master with knowledge and practice.

In the first part of the chapter, you learned seven general strategies for preparing for exams. You also learned some preparation methods for the specific kinds of exams that you'll be most likely to take in college—objective (especially multiple-choice), problem-solving, and essay. Skill Builders 10 and 11 provided additional tips along with two worksheets that can help you organize your preparation for exams.

The second part of the chapter focused on how to take exams. You read some general suggestions for improving your skills in taking examinations of all kinds. Then, you considered ideas tailored to taking different types of exams. Skill Builder 12 had you apply your knowledge to a task that's crucial for success in many college courses—understanding some of the key verbs used in essay exam questions.

Progress Check

The following questions will give you a chance to check your mastery of what you've learned about preparing for and taking examinations. Choose the best answer for each of the six questions. As usual, try to answer the questions from memory. If you've forgotten something, go back through the chapter to find the information you need. Be sure to answer all of the questions.

1. What is the best way to do your reading assignments?

- **A.** Read all at once, just before an examination
- **B.** Read one at a time, just before each is lectured on in class
- **C.** Read one at a time, just after each is lectured on in class

2. Why is it a good idea not to talk about an examination when you arrive at the exam room?

- **A.** Someone might say something that starts you worrying about a topic that you haven't prepared for.
- **B.** The instructor might consider it giving or receiving assistance.
- **C.** You might help a student less prepared than you get a better grade.

3. What topics should you spend the most time on when you study for an exam?

- **A.** All topics equally
- **B.** Most time on the topics that are easiest for you
- **C.** Most time on the topics that are hardest for you

4. Which of the following procedures probably would give you the best results on an essay exam?

- **A.** Read all questions before you start; make outlines of your answers; don't exceed two pages per answer.
- **B.** Understand what each question asks you to do; make outlines of your answers; stick to the topics.
- **C.** Make outlines of your answers; write with a highly polished style; check your work.

5. Should you look over returned exams in a course and, when they're available, the instructor's exams from the previous year? Why or why not?

A. Yes; the instructor may use many of the same questions again.
B. No; you should spend all of your time studying your text and class notes.
C. Yes; you can learn what kinds of questions the instructor likes to ask.

6. When should you complete your final review for an examination?

A. The night before the exam
B. Just before the exam begins
C. At least three days before the exam

The best answers are: **1-B; 2-A; 3-C; 4-B; 5-C; 6-A.** Could you answer all of them without looking back at the text?

Next Steps

The best way to be sure that you're making good use of the skills that you've acquired in this chapter—and in the previous four chapters—is to review each exam as soon as your instructor grades and returns it to you. Earlier, you learned that there are three important areas you can gain information about by reviewing returned exams. The three areas are your knowledge of the subject matter, your effectiveness in preparing for exams, and your effectiveness in taking exams. When you stop to think about it, you'll realize that those are among the factors that determine your chances for academic success in college.

As you progress through college, make it your habit to actively *study* returned examinations. Understanding the mistakes you make—and eliminating them in the future—can help you do a little better at showing what you've learned each time you take an exam in college. As you put haphazard preparation behind you and get past the need for last-minute cramming, you'll feel more relaxed and confident about exams. With steady practice, you should also find that your grades are beginning to improve.

Conclusion

Whether you've been using this book on your own or in a study skills course or workshop, keep it and review it frequently. Don't feel that you have to master all of the study suggestions at once. Choose only a few at a time and apply them in the general areas (for instance, reading textbooks), or in the specific courses, where you most need to build your study skills, habits, or attitudes.

As your performance begins to improve, return to this book for more suggestions. Don't forget the extra forms and worksheets in Appendix A. Make as many photocopies as you need and use them to keep yourself organized and on track for success.

Throughout the preceding five chapters, one focus has been on the fact that acquiring a college education is a process that must begin at the start of the academic term and continue daily; it can't be left until a week or so before a major exam or due date. You could almost say that's the central message of this book. It's certainly among the keys to achieving personal satisfaction and academic success in college. Keep it in mind as you progress through college. Also try to remember that, although grades are important, the *purpose* of going to college is to learn something that will make your life better. This book has gotten you off to a good start and can help you the rest of the way. *Best wishes!*

Appendix A

Extra Worksheets and Other Forms

Skill Builder 1, Chapter 1

Daily Activity List for ______________________
day

MUST DO!

1. ______________________
2. ______________________
3. ______________________
4. ______________________
5. ______________________
6. ______________________
7. ______________________
8. ______________________

SHOULD DO

1. ______________________
2. ______________________
3. ______________________
4. ______________________
5. ______________________
6. ______________________
7. ______________________
8. ______________________

COULD DO

1. ______________________
2. ______________________
3. ______________________
4. ______________________
5. ______________________
6. ______________________
7. ______________________
8. ______________________

Skill Builder 1, Chapter 1

Daily Activity List for ______________________
day

MUST DO!

1. ______________________
2. ______________________
3. ______________________
4. ______________________
5. ______________________
6. ______________________
7. ______________________
8. ______________________

SHOULD DO

1. ______________________
2. ______________________
3. ______________________
4. ______________________
5. ______________________
6. ______________________
7. ______________________
8. ______________________

COULD DO

1. ______________________
2. ______________________
3. ______________________
4. ______________________
5. ______________________
6. ______________________
7. ______________________
8. ______________________

Skill Builder 2, Chapter 1

Weekly Activity Schedule

Name ______________________________ Date ______________

Time	Monday	Tuesday	Wednesday	Thursday	Friday	Saturday	Sunday	Time
6:00 6:30								6:00 6:30
7:00 7:30								7:00 7:30
8:00 8:30								8:00 8:30
9:00 9:30								9:00 9:30
10:00 10:30								10:00 10:30
11:00 11:30								11:00 11:30
12:00 12:30								12:00 12:30
1:00 1:30								1:00 1:30
2:00 2:30								2:00 2:30
3:00 3:30								3:00 3:30
4:00 4:30								4:00 4:30
5:00 5:30								5:00 5:30
6:00 6:30								6:00 6:30
7:00 7:30								7:00 7:30
8:00 8:30								8:00 8:30
9:00 9:30								9:00 9:30
10:00 10:30								10:00 10:30

Skill Builder 2, Chapter 1

Weekly Activity Schedule

Name ______________________ Date ______________

Time	Monday	Tuesday	Wednesday	Thursday	Friday	Saturday	Sunday	Time
6:00 6:30								6:00 6:30
7:00 7:30								7:00 7:30
8:00 8:30								8:00 8:30
9:00 9:30								9:00 9:30
10:00 10:30								10:00 10:30
11:00 11:30								11:00 11:30
12:00 12:30								12:00 12:30
1:00 1:30								1:00 1:30
2:00 2:30								2:00 2:30
3:00 3:30								3:00 3:30
4:00 4:30								4:00 4:30
5:00 5:30								5:00 5:30
6:00 6:30								6:00 6:30
7:00 7:30								7:00 7:30
8:00 8:30								8:00 8:30
9:00 9:30								9:00 9:30
10:00 10:30								10:00 10:30

Skill Builder 9, Chapter 4

Research Paper Worksheet

YES	?	NO	**1.** Is your topic appropriate and relevant to the assignment?
YES	?	NO	**2.** Is your topic interesting and significant?
YES	?	NO	**3.** Is your topic focused as a question, issue, or problem?
YES	?	NO	**4.** Is your title accurate, concise, and effective?
YES	?	NO	**5.** Does your introduction capture the reader's attention?
YES	?	NO	**6.** Does your introduction clearly state the central idea?
YES	?	NO	**7.** Is your approach original and imaginative?
YES	?	NO	**8.** Is your choice of words precise and appropriate?
YES	?	NO	**9.** Are your sentences clear and effective?
YES	?	NO	**10.** Are your paragraphs unified and coherent?
YES	?	NO	**11.** Do your paragraphs follow one another logically and smoothly?
YES	?	NO	**12.** Are your ideas organized into a logical sequence?
YES	?	NO	**13.** Are your ideas supported with effective examples, quotations, etc.?
YES	?	NO	**14.** Is your presentation objective and unbiased?
YES	?	NO	**15.** Is your punctuation accurate and appropriate?
YES	?	NO	**16.** Is your spelling correct?
YES	?	NO	**17.** Is your capitalization correct and consistent?
YES	?	NO	**18.** Is your grammar correct and appropriate?
YES	?	NO	**19.** Are your sources fully and accurately identified?
YES	?	NO	**20.** Are your acknowledgments in proper form?
YES	?	NO	**21.** Are your page references correct?
YES	?	NO	**22.** Have you used quote marks for all direct quotations?
YES	?	NO	**23.** Is your bibliography or reference list complete, accurate, and in proper form?
YES	?	NO	**24.** Has your reading and observing been honestly reported?
YES	?	NO	**25.** Is your paper free of overused or repetitious words and phrases?
YES	?	NO	**26.** Is your paper free of slang and clichés?
YES	?	NO	**27.** Have your main points been summarized at the end?
YES	?	NO	**28.** Are your conclusions justified and appropriate?
YES	?	NO	**29.** Has your question, issue, or problem been effectively dealt with?
YES	?	NO	**30.** Has your paper been proofread for errors?
YES	?	NO	**31.** Are your pages numbered and do they have adequate margins?
YES	?	NO	**32.** Is your paper neat, clean, and legible?
___	___	___	

TOTALS

Skill Builder 9, Chapter 4

Research Paper Worksheet

YES	?	NO	**1.** Is your topic appropriate and relevant to the assignment?
YES	?	NO	**2.** Is your topic interesting and significant?
YES	?	NO	**3.** Is your topic focused as a question, issue, or problem?
YES	?	NO	**4.** Is your title accurate, concise, and effective?
YES	?	NO	**5.** Does your introduction capture the reader's attention?
YES	?	NO	**6.** Does your introduction clearly state the central idea?
YES	?	NO	**7.** Is your approach original and imaginative?
YES	?	NO	**8.** Is your choice of words precise and appropriate?
YES	?	NO	**9.** Are your sentences clear and effective?
YES	?	NO	**10.** Are your paragraphs unified and coherent?
YES	?	NO	**11.** Do your paragraphs follow one another logically and smoothly?
YES	?	NO	**12.** Are your ideas organized into a logical sequence?
YES	?	NO	**13.** Are your ideas supported with effective examples, quotations, etc.?
YES	?	NO	**14.** Is your presentation objective and unbiased?
YES	?	NO	**15.** Is your punctuation accurate and appropriate?
YES	?	NO	**16.** Is your spelling correct?
YES	?	NO	**17.** Is your capitalization correct and consistent?
YES	?	NO	**18.** Is your grammar correct and appropriate?
YES	?	NO	**19.** Are your sources fully and accurately identified?
YES	?	NO	**20.** Are your acknowledgments in proper form?
YES	?	NO	**21.** Are your page references correct?
YES	?	NO	**22.** Have you used quote marks for all direct quotations?
YES	?	NO	**23.** Is your bibliography or reference list complete, accurate, and in proper form?
YES	?	NO	**24.** Has your reading and observing been honestly reported?
YES	?	NO	**25.** Is your paper free of overused or repetitious words and phrases?
YES	?	NO	**26.** Is your paper free of slang and clichés?
YES	?	NO	**27.** Have your main points been summarized at the end?
YES	?	NO	**28.** Are your conclusions justified and appropriate?
YES	?	NO	**29.** Has your question, issue, or problem been effectively dealt with?
YES	?	NO	**30.** Has your paper been proofread for errors?
YES	?	NO	**31.** Are your pages numbered and do they have adequate margins?
YES	?	NO	**32.** Is your paper neat, clean, and legible?
___	___	___	

TOTALS

Skill Builder 10, Chapter 5

Exam Preparation Worksheet

1. Exam Information

Course name and section ______________________________

Day, date, time, and place of exam ______________________________

Kind of exam
___ Essay ___ Multiple-choice ___ True-false
___ Short answer ___ Problem-solving ___ Other

Amount of time allowed for exam ______________________________

"Weight" of exam in total grade for course (if known) ____________ %

Textbook chapter(s) or pages covered on exam ______________________________

____

____

Lecture or discussion topics covered on exam ______________________________

____

____

Other material or activities covered on exam (films or videotapes, lab experiments or demonstrations, etc.) ______________________________

____

2. Study Completion Schedule

STUDY ACTIVITY	DEADLINE
Textbook chapter(s) or pages to read ____________ ______________________________	____________
Lecture or discussion notes to correct, expand, or (if missing) copy from a classmate ____________ ______________________________	____________
Other materials or activities to finish ____________ ______________________________	____________

3. Review Schedule

REVIEW ACTIVITY	DEADLINE
Review textbook chapter(s) or pages	____________
Review lecture or discussion notes	____________
Compare textbook material with class notes	____________
Review other materials or activities	____________
Review with small group of other students (optional)	____________

Skill Builder 10, Chapter 5

Exam Preparation Worksheet

1. Exam Information

Course name and section ____________________

Day, date, time, and place of exam ____________________

Kind of exam ___ Essay ___ Multiple-choice ___ True-false
___ Short answer ___ Problem-solving ___ Other

Amount of time allowed for exam ____________________

"Weight" of exam in total grade for course (if known) __________ %

Textbook chapter(s) or pages covered on exam ____________________

____

____

Lecture or discussion topics covered on exam ____________________

____

____

Other material or activities covered on exam (films or videotapes, lab experiments or demonstrations, etc.) ____________________

____

2. Study Completion Schedule

STUDY ACTIVITY	DEADLINE
Textbook chapter(s) or pages to read ______ ____________________	__________
Lecture or discussion notes to correct, expand, or (if missing) copy from a classmate ______ ____________________	__________
Other materials or activities to finish ______ ____________________	__________

3. Review Schedule

REVIEW ACTIVITY	DEADLINE
Review textbook chapter(s) or pages	__________
Review lecture or discussion notes	__________
Compare textbook material with class notes	__________
Review other materials or activities	__________
Review with small group of other students (optional)	__________

Skill Builder 11, Chapter 5

No. ____ of ____

Essay Exam Worksheet

Essay Question and Source: ______________________________

____

____

____

Answer: ______________________________

____

____

____

____

____

____

____

____

____

____

____

____

____

____

____

____

____

____

____

____

____

____

____

____

____

Skill Builder 11, Chapter 5

No. _____ of _____

Essay Exam Worksheet

Essay Question and Source: ____

Answer: ____

Appendix B

Answer Keys

Skill Builder 5, Chapter 2

PASSAGE #1

LANDING A SMALL AIRPLANE

A pilot must follow a strict sequence of three steps in landing a small plane. These three steps, though simple enough in themselves, must always occur in the correct order.

Turn on the Carburetor Heat

The first step is to turn on the carburetor heat. This is essential because the next step, pulling back on the throttle, could otherwise cause freezing in the carburetor, which could cause a complete loss of power. Thus, turning on the carburetor heat is a very important first step.

Pull Back on the Throttle

The pilot then pulls back on the throttle and raises the nose of the plane. This reduces the airspeed, which must be done before taking the next step, lowering the flaps on the wings. Failure to reduce the airspeed before lowering the flaps could cause enough stress on the wings to result in structural damage. Needless to say, any structural damage to the wings is potentially dangerous.

Lower the Flaps

After reducing the airspeed, the pilot lowers the flaps. This makes it possible for the plane to sustain flight at a lower airspeed, which makes landing safer.

PASSAGE #2

REFRIGERATION

Characteristics of a Gas

Temperature changes often accompany the compression or expansion of a gas. Modern refrigeration is made possible as a result of these changes.

Compression Increases Temperature

In the case of compression, the temperatures of most gases increase. Under some circumstances, the temperature change can be large enough to initiate a chemical reaction. One effective demonstration of this is the "fire stick," a tube with a hand plunger for compressing the air. If a wisp of cotton is placed in the bottom of the tube and the air is rapidly compressed, the cotton will burn with a flash. The same effect is responsible for the operation of the diesel engine, which, unlike the gasoline engine, does not have a spark plug to trigger combustion when the engine is running.

Expansion Decreases Temperature

If a compressed gas is allowed to expand, the opposite effect results; the temperature of the gas decreases. On a small scale, this occurs when air is released from a tire. On a larger scale, it occurs when a mass of air rises; as the mass of air ascends, it expands because the surrounding pressure decreases. The consequent temperature drop may be so large that the moisture in the air condenses to form a cloud.

Use of Gas in Refrigeration

Both compression and expansion principles are used in the design of the refrigerator. In a refrigerator, a gas circulates in a closed loop that includes a compressor (placed outside the refrigerator to compress the gas) and 2 sets of coils for heat transfer (1 inside and 1 outside the refrigerator). If a compressed gas is allowed to expand immediately, it simply cools to its original temperature. However, if the warm gas is first allowed to cool somewhat (by passing it through the coils outside the refrigerator), any subsequent expansion of the gas results in a gas at a temperature lower than the original temperature.

A substance that remains in the gaseous phase throughout this compression-expansion cycle transfers only a small amount of heat in each cycle. Considerably more heat is released when a gas is compressed to a liquid than when a gas is compressed to a denser gas. Thus the refrigeration process is made efficient by using a gas that condenses to a liquid when it is compressed; a large amount of heat is therefore released in each cycle of refrigerator operation.

PASSAGE #3

GROSS NATIONAL PRODUCT: A KEY ECONOMIC INDICATOR

One widely used indicator of the nation's yearly economic performance is **Gross National Product,** or **GNP.** To understand the importance of GNP as an economic indicator, it is necessary to examine what GNP measures and how it reflects the status of the major sectors of the economy.

The Scope of GNP

Gross National Product measures the total dollar value of all final **goods** (for example, a loaf of bread or a television) and **services** (for example, a haircut or a medical check-up) produced in America during a given year. Calculated and announced annually by the U.S. Department of Commerce, GNP is expressed in numbers so large as to be meaningful only to trained economists and statisticians. In recent years, GNP volume has grown into the trillions of dollars.

It should be noted that the Commerce Department includes in GNP only the value of **final** goods and services. **Intermediate** goods and services (those used in the production of final goods and services) are not counted in the GNP calculation. The reason for this distinction is that the value of final goods and services includes the value of all intermediate goods and services used in their production. Thus, for example, the value of a loaf of bread (a final good) would be counted in GNP, but the value of the flour and other ingredients (intermediate goods) used in making it would not be counted.

The Components of GNP

One way of calculating GNP is to add up expenditures for final goods and services that were produced in the U.S. during the year. In calculating GNP by this method, the Commerce Department analyzes the expenditures of the four sectors of the economy that buy goods and services: **private consumers, business and industry, government,** and **foreign interests.** From year to year, each of these groups adjusts its purchasing behavior in response to the actual or expected economic conditions that it is subject to, producing positive or negative effects on GNP.

Expenditures by Private Consumers

Private consumers, both households and individuals, make up the largest of the four sectors of the economy, and their expenditures constitute the largest component of GNP. The personal consumption of households and individuals accounts for almost two-thirds of all goods and services purchased. Private consumers allocate their purchases according to their personal financial circumstances and the state of the economy.

For example, when their incomes rise, consumers tend to buy relatively more **durable goods,** such as cars and washing machines, rather than **nondurable goods,** such as clothing and groceries. Compared to the other components of GNP, the overall level of consumer spending is more stable from year to year.

Expenditures by Business and Industry

The expenditures of business and industry make up the most volatile component of GNP. This is because, while consumers must spend money on basic necessities like food, clothing, and housing regardless of income levels or prices, the business sector of the economy has the option of postponing the construction of a new factory or the purchase of new machinery when economic conditions are unfavorable. Typically, businesses invest in expansion or improvements when they expect the economy to perform well and defer such investment when they expect the economy to be sluggish.

Expenditures by Government

A third component of GNP is government expenditures. The kinds of goods and services purchased vary considerably at each of the three levels of the government sector of the economy: **federal, state,** and **local.** For example, state and local governments spend proportionately more on the education of their citizens than does the federal government. Indeed, for some state and local governments, education is the single most expensive item in their budgets. A continued decline in the number of school-aged children might slow the growth of expenditures for education and thus reduce the positive impact on GNP of state and local government spending.

Expenditures by Foreign Interests

The fourth component of GNP is the expenditures of the various foreign interests that purchase American goods and services. The foreign-based sector of the economy includes both governments and business and industry. Foreign purchases tend to center most heavily on high-technology items, such as electronic communications equipment and military weapons systems, and basic foodstuffs, such as wheat and other grains. Gross national product is positively affected when the United States sells more to foreign interests than it buys from them.

Progress Check, Chapter 2

1. List three of the signal words and phrases that textbook authors use to help students follow the information being presented. Briefly explain what each of your choices means.

- Introductory signals: "The chief cause," "The three major factors," "Historically, the five underlying conditions"
- Relational signals: "First . . . , Second . . . , Third . . ."; "In addition," "Moreover," "Furthermore"; "Likewise," "By the same token"; "However," "Nevertheless," "Conversely," "On the other hand"
- Conclusive signals: "Thus," "Therefore," "Consequently," "In the final analysis"

2. What are the two kinds of typographical emphasis most commonly used in textbooks to make a key point stand out or to introduce a new word or concept?

- Italic type
- Boldface type

3. Name four kinds of visual aids that are often used in textbooks.

- Photographs
- Cartoons
- Diagrams and other drawings
- Maps
- Graphs
- Charts
- Tables

4. What are three of the parts or features that may be included in the back matter of a textbook?

- Appendix
- Glossary
- Bibliography
- Index

5. State two ways of clarifying or going beyond the information in a textbook.

- Participate in class discussions.
- Ask questions during or after lectures.
- See instructor for recommendations about supplemental readings.
- Research topic(s) in college library.

6. What are the five steps, in order, of the SQ3R Reading Method?

- 1. Survey
- 2. Question
- 3. Read
- 4. Recite
- 5. Review

7. Name three of the one-word questions that can help you in turning textbook headings into questions.

- Who?
- What?
- When?
- Where?
- Why?
- How?

8. What does the word "recite" mean to you?

- Restating the main points of a reading assignment in your own words, without looking at the text

Skill Builder 6, Chapter 3

Outlining Worksheet

Types of Sports

Baseball	Individual Sports	Table Sports
Bicycling	Jogging	Team Sports
Contact Sports	Land Sports	Tennis
Court Sports	Noncontact Sports	Track and Field
Diving	Ping-Pong	Two- and Four-Person Sports
Football	Pool/Billiards	Volleyball
Handball/Racquetball	Soccer/Rugby	Water Sports
Hiking	Surfing	
Hockey	Swimming	

I. Individual Sports
  A. Land Sports
    1. Bicycling
    2. Hiking
    3. Jogging
  B. Water Sports
    1. Diving
    2. Surfing
    3. Swimming

II. Two- and Four-Person Sports
  A. Court Sports
    1. Handball/Racquetball
    2. Tennis
  B. Table Sports
    1. Ping-Pong
    2. Pool/Billiards

III. Team Sports
  A. Contact Sports
    1. Football
    2. Hockey
    3. Soccer/Rugby
  B. Noncontact Sports
    1. Baseball
    2. Track and Field
    3. Volleyball

Skill Builder 7, Chapter 3

Oral Signals Worksheet

Signal Words and Phrases

a case in point	furthermore	on the other hand
additionally	however	similarly
by the same token	in conclusion	therefore
consequently	in the final analysis	thus
conversely	likewise	to illustrate
for instance	moreover	to summarize

Signals indicating a continuation and expansion	Signals indicating an example
additionally	a case in point
furthermore	for instance
moreover	to illustrate

Signals indicating a parallel	Signals indicating a difference or exception
by the same token	conversely
likewise	however
similarly	on the other hand

Signals indicating a specific result or effect	Signals indicating a general wrap-up or review
consequently	in conclusion
therefore	in the final analysis
thus	to summarize

Progress Check, Chapter 3

1. What are the four features that all effective note taking systems have in common?

- They *highlight* the main ideas covered in a class session.
- They *show the relationships* among the main ideas.
- They *organize* the minor points, details, facts, etc.
- They *remind you* of your assignments and due dates.

2. Name three ways of keeping alert in class and maintaining your concentration.

- Focus your attention on the information being presented.
- Make a commitment to understand, write down, and remember the main points.
- Choose a seat where you can hear and see well.
- Put distracting thoughts out of mind.
- Skim your notes just before the start of a class.
- Listen actively for answers to questions that you thought of earlier.
- Listen both to learn the material and to identify possible exam questions.
- Participate in class discussions.
- Change position if you start getting restless or drowsy.

3. At what rate, in words per minute, do people mentally process spoken information that they hear? What's the fastest rate at which instructors usually deliver lectures?

- 400 words per minute
- 100 words per minute

4. Name three of the shortcuts you can use in class to make note taking simpler.

- Be selective about what you write down.
- Write notes in sentence fragments.
- Use abbreviations and symbols.

5. What are four of the signal words or phrases that college instructors use to help students trace the connections among ideas in lectures and class discussions?

- "Consequently"
- "Therefore"
- "Conversely"
- "Furthermore"
- "Likewise"
- "On the other hand"
- "To illustrate"
- "To summarize," etc.

6. Describe three of the things students can do to improve their notes when editing and reviewing them after class.

- Fill in areas where notes are sketchy and incomplete.
- Clarify abbreviations.
- Correct errors.
- Add omitted material and, if helpful, material from textbook.
- Underline or highlight main concepts, terms, and facts.

7. What does the word "cross-referencing" mean to you?

- Comparing class notes with reading assignments and integrating the two

Skill Builder 12, Chapter 5

Key Verbs Worksheet

__F__ **1.** Compare

__C__ **2.** Contrast

__I__ **3.** Criticize or Evaluate

__B__ **4.** Define

__H__ **5.** Describe, Discuss, or Explain

__E__ **6.** Illustrate

__A__ **7.** List, Outline, or Summarize

__D__ **8.** Prove

__G__ **9.** Trace

A. Briefly state main points, facts, ideas, or concepts

B. State the meaning of a word or concept

C. State the differences between or among things, ideas, events, or problems

D. Demonstrate that something is true by giving factual evidence or logical reasons

E. Use analogies or examples to tell about or clarify a point or problem

F. State the similarities between or among things, ideas, events, or problems

G. State the progress, development, or history of something in chronological order

H. Give a complete, balanced overview of a topic, with details

I. State your view or opinion on a subject, giving facts or reasons

Index